Tastes and Tales
of New York's Southern Tier

Tastes and Tales
of New York's Southern Tier

Profiles and recipes from leading restaurants...
A glance back at eateries from days gone by...
And an in-depth look at Spiedies....

Paul C. VanSavage
With Suzanne M. Meredith and Ed Aswad

Foreword by Chef Carmen Quagliata
Introduction by Don Giovanni

J.E.T. Creative Media
265 Main Street
Binghamton, NY 13905

Published by
J.E.T. Creative Media
265 Main Street
Binghamton, New York 13905

Although the author and publisher have made every effort to ensure the accuracy and completeness of information contained in this book, we assume no responsibility for errors, inaccuracies, omissions, or any inconsistency herein. Any slights of people, places or organizations are unintentional.

First printing 2006
Second printing 2007

Associate Writer - Suzanne M. Meredith
Editor - Angelo Zuccolo
Cover and text design - Robb Gomulka
Photography - Ed Aswad
          Carriage House Photography
Published by Paul Battisti
          J.E.T. Creative Media

ISBN 1-891444-13-1

Attention: Businesses and Not-For-Profit Agencies

Quantity discounts are available on bulk purchases of this book for resale, business or sales incentives, or for fund-raising purposes. For more information, please contact J.E.T. Creative Media, 265 Main Street, Binghamton, NY 13905

Acknowledgements
Paul VanSavage

My first step with this project was to find a good Publisher and fortune led me to Paul Battisti at Jet Creative Media. From the first time we met, Paul has not only provided the technical publishing support that I needed, but his unbridled enthusiasm kept me motivated.

Then it was time to put together the team. We first contacted the accomplished writer, Suzanne Meredith. She shared our enthusiasm for the book and has done an outstanding job polishing my work. Angelo Zuccolo, another published author, agreed to edit the material. His attention to detail is unsurpassed. When it came time to select a photographer, who else but Ed Aswad? In addition to his renowned skills as a photographer, his experience in authoring and co-authoring books was invaluable. And finally, Robb Gomulka exceeded our expectations with a cover design that we feel is outstanding.

A number of other people were extremely helpful in providing information on businesses from the past and leads for other sources. They include Joe Pisani, John Dellos, Anthony Iacovelli, Jane Zades, Patricia Zades Loposky, Rocco DeSisto, Frank DeRosa, Beth Putrino, Lisa Temple, Jim Iacovelli, Barbara Oldwine, Lena Bishop, Jim and Carol Herz, George and Nancy Yezzi, and Linda Felton Shelton.

The Broome County Historical Society was a tremendous resource, both from the standpoint of its research materials and providing copies of old photographs.

Wendy Thibeault and the organizers of the Central New York Maple Festival were outstanding in providing information on the Festival.

Charlie Quagliata put us in touch with his nephew, Carmen, who has written the Foreword and his brother, John, who has made his mark with a national chain of restaurants.

A special thanks to Carmen for his willingness to take time from his busy schedule at the Union Square Café to write the Foreword and to Don Giovanni, the noted radio personality, who wrote the Introduction.

Debbie Morello and the BCC ExCEL Program provided outstanding guidance and introduced me to Cheryl Fabrizi, who shared her wealth of marketing experience, and helped guide the creation of the Website and overall marketing plan.

This book would not have been possible without the cooperation from the dozens of business owners who took time away from hectic schedules to be interviewed. Without them there would be no book.

My sister, Helen White, who knows more about selling books than anyone else I know, was always there with advice and provided a wonderful sounding-board.

Whenever I've come up with crazy ideas through the years (and there have been quite a few), my family has always been completely supportive. My son, Rich, provided constant encouragement and advice, and my daughters and their husbands, Michelle and Fred Larsh and Kate and Dave Prybyla, gave me invaluable feedback and advice.

Last, but by no means least, is my wife Ann. Without her unconditional and enthusiastic support, I could not have even started the project. Her objective guidance was always there when I needed it most, and I'll always be grateful.

This is your book, Southern Tier. I have enjoyed every moment of the process in bringing it to you.

Author's preface
Paul VanSavage

Some might call me a food enthusiast; others say I'm food-centric; I just call myself a "Foodie". I also have a tremendous respect for anyone operating a small business, especially one that's food related. That combination of my love for food and my respect for small business operators led me to writing this book.

It's been my good fortune to have had many opportunities throughout my working career, including a stint at the Holiday Inn-Arena, where I had my first exposure to a commercial kitchen. I was able to see first-hand the organized chaos that goes on in a restaurant kitchen. Just think about the timing that a chef must consider. Suppose that a couple places their order, one for seared scallops and the other for broiled, double-cut pork chops. One takes ninety seconds and the other eleven minutes, but they must come out to the server at exactly the same time. Or, consider the table of eight, all ordering the same dish, requiring the preparation of a special sauce that's made to order for each dish; imagine the swirl of sauté pans.

But operating a restaurant isn't just a matter of serving good food. The owner must be a purchasing genius, human resources expert, facilities manager, and public relations guru, all wrapped into one. And it doesn't hurt to know how to cook on top of it.

When I first started to make a list of the locally-owned restaurants, diners and food related businesses operating in the Southern Tier, I was astounded at the number. It's especially true when you take into consideration the deluge of chain restaurants that have permeated our community in recent years. As I interviewed owners and chefs, I tried to capture the history of the establishment; the personality of the owner, which is usually reflected in the business, and some insight regarding their successes.

At the same time, it was rather sad to review the long list of restaurants that are no longer in business. So many great places have gone by the wayside for a variety of reasons. Some were displaced by highways, some simply outlived their original owners, and others couldn't compete in the ever-changing food industry.

Writing this book has been a joy. The dozens of people whom I interviewed were all a delight to chat with, and I feel like I've made many new friends.

I can sum up the entire process with one of my favorite sayings by Virginia Woolf: "One cannot think well, love well, sleep well, if one has not dined well."

Doesn't that say it all?

Contents

Foreword
Chef Carmen Quagliata

Since I left the Triple Cities almost twenty years ago to build a career as a professional chef, not a day has gone by where my childhood of eating and cooking in the Triple Cities has not somehow influenced who I am.

My first memories of what would become a lifelong love affair with food came through my family's summer picnics to Chenango Valley State Park in the mid seventies. It was there that I ate or remember eating my first Spiedies and my grandparents' homemade sausages. While growing up, what we ate always seemed so important, so central to the day, season or celebration. My brother, two sisters and I would always tell my mom how great dinner was and that she should open her own restaurant which must have been nice to hear since she was a single mom raising 4 kids. It usually put a smile on her face. There were oohs, aahs and mmm's over a simple bowl of pasta e lenticchie (lentils). Or, with hunks of bread in hand, we would fight for the last dip of the garlic flecked, bloody juice from a London broil. Of course Sundays at my grandmothers' table would initiate the same discussion and reverence about the meal happily being savored.

Besides the picnics, home meals, and relatives' meals, there were the restaurant adventures. Going out to eat was always exciting. Thinking and talking about what to order would fill the car ride to the restaurant. Whether it be Cortese after a hockey game, Little Venice, Tony's (where as a Middle and High School student in the '80's you could get 2 slices and a coke for a $1.25), Oaks Inn (where I had a near perfect meal on one of my trips home a few years back), or any of the many other restaurants we would go to, the anticipation of getting a scrumptious plate of food that so easily appeared from beyond those swinging kitchen doors made me happy. (It also made me curious about how they did it so well; but, more on that later.) The really special places were Orlando's, Lacanda Pepina, Number 5 and Surf 'n Turf. There were others but those are the ones that stand out in my mind.

I remember when I finally ate at Orlando's. It was such a big deal. Everybody always talked about Orlando's and after I took my first bite of my veal saltimbocca I knew why. The sauce with the veal was like I never had before. The bread was warm, crunchy and at the same time chewy, the salad greens were colder and crisper. Nothing against the other places we frequented at the time, but it was the first time I realized there were different types of dining experiences to explore.

During my pre-teen and adolescent years there were experiences that further reinforced my passion for food. Probably the most prominent of those experiences that played out hundreds of times for me, and I'm sure a majority of the people I know, is pizza. Now, for any fellow foodies and chefs (professional or accomplished home chefs) reading this, please do not view me as unsophisticated. After all, is there anything more full flavored, more satisfying, more revered by more people than a bite of pizza?

Having grown up on the North Side of Endicott in the 1980's I am convinced that my generation are connoisseurs of, and witnesses to, the North Side "Sheet Pizza" Golden Age. The Pax Romana of the Pie you might say. There was Ron DeVita's market on Squires Ave., Rossi's on Oak Hill and Nirchi's on Pine St. There were a few others in the 'hood but we'll stick to those major players. On any given day of....I guess you could say the "Stand By Me" years of my boyhood, me, my brother and our friends were constantly getting a slice (in between baseball games or whatever mischief we were up to) from any one of these corner markets. Not to mention the Friday nights that, separately in our own homes, we would have sheet pizza for dinner. There were discussions of where to get the pizza from tonight and debates about the pros and cons of each: Was Rossi's too greasy? DeVita's not enough stuff? Nirchi's too runny? I was never arguing. I liked them all. Like a budding connoisseur of food I was crafty and patient. You had to get the white Pizza at DeVita's (I was partial to their crust also). Rossi's you had to eat right away while it was hot. And Nirchi's… if you had the will power, everyone knows Nirchi's had to rest, settle in on itself and cool down. Nirchi's seemed to be a controversial pie to love for those of the Triple Cities not from Endicott. But we North Siders will tell you, Nirchi's could possibly be the best morning after breakfast Pizza ever!

As life moved on to the Middle school years we were able to take advantage of "off campus lunch" There was, as I mentioned, the ever popular Tony's pizza, but if you walked in the opposite direction of Jenny F Snapp Middle School towards Nanticoke Ave you would stumble upon Jim Roma's bakery.

I used to think how lucky we were to be getting his bread, fresh out of the oven. On good days, we would continue across the street to the Cider Mill and get warm donuts right off the conveyor belt with fresh pressed apple cider. This is when I probably realized fresh meant everything… a good lesson for someone developing a real interest in food.

Then came Duff's and Brother's 2 in the high school years. Both favorite post CYO basketball game haunts. Duff's was on the lower North Side and had a very thin crust pizza with just the right amount of cheese and a bright fresh tasting sauce. The later high school years found us frequently parked at a booth at Brothers 2 on Watson Blvd. for their Pizza and extra hot wings.

Other than my grandmother's Friday Sicilian Pizza (very little or no Mozzarella, just great sauce, oregano and Pecorino cheese) the most influential Pizza I can remember outside of Endicott was Cortese pizza. I have had many bowls of the gnocchi at Cortese but what stood out for me was the cakey crusted thick pizza with a bowl of tossed salad and blue cheese dressing. It's fitting to close my possibly too long pizza rant with a little quote from my wife Palma. On our first trip to the Triple Cities to meet my family I had to go and get all the foods from all the places (including the home cooked ones) that I loved. To the dismay of my soon to be wife, many of those stops included pizza, wings and Spiedies. Ever since that trip 11 years ago, every time we set a date to take a trip home with our boys she announces "Boys no pizza for you and your father for a month, we're going to Binghamton soon."

When I was 16 I started working at Banquet Masters next to Union Endicott High School for Bucky Picciano and Chef Bob Grencer. It was there in the pressurized kitchen of Banquet Masters that I realized I wanted to become a career chef. Throughout the long, hard summer days learning from Chef Grencer he would turn to me and ask, "So you want to be a chef?" and wink. I knew the answer and I never gave up trying to impress him. I must have done OK, because Chef and Mr. Picciano wrote me letters of recommendation to the Culinary Institute of America (where Chef Grencer also received his formal training). I am very proud to have worked at Banquet Masters. It may have been a tough job, but everyone had high expectations of each other and Bucky, Bob and Tara Picciano (the service manager) made those expectations clear to everyone. It was my first job in the business and I was lucky enough to be part of an establishment that cared and was striving for excellent customer service. I really remember the guests being very happy. Whether it was a wedding for 400 on Saturday night or a Rotary Club meeting on Wednesday afternoon, Banquet Masters seemed to make people happy. And, I was learning another lesson that would help build my career.

Once I had applied to the CIA, my Uncle Charles Quagliata and I went on a trip to tour the campus and eat lunch in the student run, fine dining French restaurant, The Escoffier Room. It was my first real introduction to dining outside of the Triple Cities and to haute cuisine. What transpired that afternoon is still one of my uncle's favorite restaurant stories. One of the courses in the lunch we ordered was escargot. The little snails were placed in front of me with a peculiar set of tools. I looked down at the plate of foreign species and the surgical equipment that accompanied thcm and then looked at my uncle. With a compassionate smile he asked, "Do you know what to do?" I promptly, without shame, answered "No." He showed me how to hold the escargot in the springy, taut holder and then how to pick out the succulent, garlicky bud of meat. I gave it a go and (it being my first time) didn't get the shell all the way in the springy device and launched my escargot half way across the dining room. I don't remember my reaction but I do remember the embarrassment of that snail sailing away from me and the big grin on my uncle's face. In spite of the minor mess of the splattered escargot, I was allowed to enroll in the CIA where I learned to cook the classics and so much more.

After the CIA I worked in The Greenbrier apprenticeship program where I put to use the basics I learned in school. I also did a stint at the Naples, Florida Ritz-Carlton. In between I worked in Cleveland, Ohio for Tower City Plaza Hotel, where I was blessed to have spent time with my Uncle John Quagliata, then President of Stouffer Restaurants. I credit him with showing me the importance of toughness and tenacity coupled with other leadership abilities to work in a challenging business where in the end you needed to turn to the customer, smile and put them at ease.

In 1991 I headed west to find my next challenge. I settled into a big beautiful restaurant in the Napa Valley with Chef Michael Chiarello called Tra Vigne. There I enjoyed the essential formative years of my career, cooking what the farms and seasons brought to our door all the while working my way up to becoming Executive Chef and finally Michael's partner.

Once, while in California, I met a nice lady, a onetime Binghamton University student who fell in love with the Spiedie while attending school. We were at a cookout and somehow Binghamton came up and then of course the Spiedie. The excitement that overcame her made me so proud. As I spoke of the generally required ingredients in the lamb and pork Spiedie marinades she bobbed her wide-eyed head up and down busting at the seams to tell me what she knew and experienced as if she were ready to scream "Yes I'm in the club too, I've been there."

Soon Lupo's came up and that's when I told her that I grew up 2 blocks from the original Lupo's market on North Rogers Ave. "No Way!" she gasped. Now my Spiedie ego was nearing a dangerous level mind you, but I couldn't help but tell her that I was the grandson of Carmelo and Giovanna Quagliata of Quality Market where copious amounts of marinated Spiedies and homemade sausages were sold for many a summer cookout in and around Binghamton for many years. That's when her jaw dropped and she told me she had friends that lived in that neighborhood and that she had eaten said delicacies. She let out a quiet and respectful "Wowww" as if to acknowledge her proximity to Spiedie royalty (Hey, I'm just a poor kid from upstate New York; It's the only chance I'll ever get to call myself royalty.) We went on to figure out that she had seen kids in the store on occasion who were most likely me and my siblings hanging out in the store as we so often did.

If our regional cuisine had a face the Spiedie would be the main feature. It would be the sexy mole near a woman's lip. It would be the square jaw on a GQ cover model. It is what I think elevates us; perhaps what gives us in the Triple Cities a slightly healthy superiority complex.

In 2001, married and with two sons in tow, we moved back east where I took over a restaurant called the Vault in downtown Boston. That experience, although successful, was fairly brief and led to my current position as Chef de Cuisine at Danny Meyer's and Michael Romano's famed Union Square Café in New York City.

This past Spring, right around the time that Paul Van Savage contacted me to be part of this project, my wife and two sons were returning from a trip to Binghamton that I couldn't join them on because of work. As the boys were giving me the rundown of their visits with Grandma and their great uncles they told me about the Pierogi lunch they had with Uncle Charlie and his friends at St. Michaels. Being half Polish from my mother's side and loving Pierogi, I was awash in memory and wished I were with them as they had their first true on site taste of the Southern Tier.

Eventually, I couldn't help but think that there are countless memories from all generations throughout the Southern Tier. Stories just like mine that shape people and give them identity. And so much of that identity is connected to the smells, textures, and taste of food...glorious food.

Ah, the stories that food history has to tell. I don't mean in levels of sophistication, but in the gusto and levels of soul. It is looking back before the recent food culture explosion that you can see the Southern Tier indeed does have a wonderful and rich history for Paul Van Savage to capture in this book. This is why we who have left stay connected to our past because we left a piece of soul that must be revisited as often as possible.

There will always be more foods to explore and untold stories to eat. My seven and five year old boys have already been to Sharkey's and the Cider Mill but have yet to have a Pat Mitchell's cone or baklava at the Greek Festival. So on we go eating… and you can be sure I'll be having Pierogies next spring at St Michaels….possibly with a copy of Tales and Tastes of the Southern Tier in hand.

I know you will enjoy this celebration of Southern Tier food….bon appetite, always!

Introduction
Don Giovanni

Paul VanSavage is one of Greater Binghamton's unsung heroes. He describes himself as a Foodie and I would also like to describe him as an idea guy.

You see, Paul had this little idea one day way back in 1983 to have a Spiedie Cooking Contest and the rest, as they say, is history. The little contest has blossomed into our area's biggest event with fun for the entire family every summer! The Spiedie Fest and Balloon Rally takes place the first weekend in August every year and raises hundreds of thousands of dollars for local charities.

Now, this self-titled Foodie has done it again by authoring this wonderful book that captures the tastes, aromas and memories in our beautiful valley. Paul shares his love of our hometown and takes us on a trip down memory lane to revisit our favorite old restaurants and markets. Some of our old, favorite places may have long since served their last patron, and turned the closed sign over in the window for the last time. But, don't be sad...Paul has the key to the door and as he paints his word pictures you are suddenly right back in your favorite booth and here comes your favorite waitress to serve you. Cherish those memories and you can always go back. The store is always open for you and good news...Paul's got the check!

If you're like me and LOVE local history, and LOVE food, you too might be a Foodie! Buon Appetito!

P.S. -- "Dear Paul, Thanks for the memories."

Restaurants and Diners

Aiello's Ristorante

Barstow House

Binghamton Club

Broadway Diner

Brothers 2 Restaurant

Bull's Head Restaurant

Chestnut Inn

Coffee Talk

Consol's Restaurant

Cortese Restaurant

Delgado's Cafe

Donoli's Restaurant

Glenmary Inn

Gramma Jo's

Hallo Berlin

J. Michael's Restaurant

Jailhouse Restaurant

Kampai Japanese Restaurant

Little Venice

Mario's Pizza

McGirk's Irish Pub

Mekong Restaurant

Mountain Top Grove

Nirchi's

Number 5 Restaurant

Oaks Inn

Olde World Deli

Our Country Hearts

Park Diner and Restaurant

Parkview Hotel

Phil's Chicken House

Plantation House

Portfolio's Café

Pronto Restaurant

PS Restaurant

Red Robin Diner

Red's Kettle Inn

Russell Steak and Seafood House

Scott's Oquaga Lake House

Sharkey's

Silo Restaurant

Southside Yanni's

Spiedie and Rib Pit

The Cellar

The Sherwood Inn

Theo's Southern Style Cuisine

Tom & Marty's Town House Restaurant

Tom's Texas Hots

Tony's Italian Grill

Uncle Tony's

Whole in the Wall Restaurant

Aiello's Ristorante
Whitney Point, NY

During World War II, Fortunato and Vincenza Signorelli Cangemi fed American troops in Sicily, but it wouldn't be the last time a member of their family would prepare food for Americans. After the war, their daughter, Giuseppa, married Vito Aiello and they moved to Brooklyn, NY. Vito made a career maintaining the United Nations building, but he always knew that one day the family would return to the restaurant business.

Throughout the years, Vito would head upstate to hunt and he'd stop in Roscoe, at his cousin Ramondo's restaurant, and then continue up Route 206 for a stop at Aiello's Restaurant in Walton to say hello to another cousin, finally arriving in Whitney Point. Every time he drove into Whitney Point he'd look at the vacant and dilapidated structure known as the Griffin Hotel and think, "Someone could really do something with that building."

He wanted to help his two sons start a business and move out of the concrete jungle of New York City. When he looked at that old building, he saw nothing but potential. Charlie was 23 and Vincenzo was 18 when Vito proposed buying the Griffin Hotel and renovating it to house what would be known as Aiello's Ristorante.

Vito spent untold hours working on the building. He preserved what was unique, like the mural depicting the Hatfield-McCoy feud, painted by William and Grant Smith. He painstakingly stripped the paint from the original wood trim in the old bar room and rebuilt the remaining restaurant.

At first, it was just a pizza parlor, like the one which their uncle operated in Brooklyn. Charlie did everything in those days; he'd answer the phone, slide the pizzas into the ovens, pull them out, cut them and ring up the sale. Business was good, so good that it was soon clear that he needed more help. That's when brother Vincenzo became a partner and brought in his own energy and ideas.

It was time to expand from a pizza and pasta place to a full-blown Italian restaurant. The brothers had a keen business sense and believed that the smartest investment which they could make would be hiring an accomplished chef. As unusual as it may seem, their first chef, Max, was from Taiwan. He was immensely talented, and you'll still find a slight Asian influence in some of the dishes served today. An example is the Aiello Chicken Wings, which are sweet and sassy with a touch of Soy Sauce.

Max was followed by a number of equally accomplished chefs, like Michael White, Thomas Rose, John Palmater and Dave Micha, all of whom have gone on to successful careers elsewhere. Today, Cosimo Summa is the head chef. He started as a dishwasher and learned from the all of the chefs with whom he worked. Vincenzo, who runs the "back of the house" while Charlie takes care of the "front of the house", is quick to say that Cosimo is the fastest chef they've had, but he never sacrifices quality to get meals out quickly.

Today their menu is extensive, including such popular offerings as Prime Rib Wellington, Penne alla Vodka with Prosciutto, Pasta con salsa di pesce, better known as Pasta with Seafood Sauces. The Mussels with Red Wine Sauce is always a hit, as is the Haddock, which is flown in from Iceland. But the big sellers are Chicken Parmigiana and Sicilian Eggplant Parmigiana. In season, fresh herbs and tomatoes come from Vito's garden.

To cater to the traveler without a lot of time for lunch, Aiello's features a lunch buffet. Patty Manzo is responsible for the traditional American favorites on the buffet, such as chicken and biscuits, meatloaf, sausages with sauerkraut, and baked ham.

Every St. Patrick's Day, the Italian brothers are banished from the kitchen by the chefs who prepare traditional Irish cuisine.

They have also added periodic Wine Pairing dinners. A six-course prix fixe dinner with wine paired to each course is offered and sells out every time it's held.

Charlie describes good wine as the nectar of the gods and maintains a very broad wine list, with selections ranging from Wagner Ice Wine to Santa Margherita Pinot Grigio to Kendall Jackson Grand Reserve Cabernet Sauvignon.

Charlie and Vincenzo are loyal customers of Maines Paper and Food Service and especially Vice-President Charlie Feldman. They credit a part of their success to knowing that Charlie is always there to assist them, even showing up in the kitchen to help prepare a new dish.

Aiello's Ristorante is truly a family affair. In addition to Charlie's wife Angela and Vincenzo's wife Maria, you'll find a number of younger Aiellos pitching in. Sons and daughters Maria, Giuseppa, Josephine, Anna, little Vito and cousin big Vito can all be found busing tables, working as servers and hostesses, and doing whatever is necessary to carry on the family business.

Charlie and Vincenzo take pride in providing healthy alternatives on the menu and have been repeatedly recognized by the American Heart Association for the Heart Healthy menu choices. They continually offer new options like multi-grain pasta, and they're experimenting with multi-grain pizza dough.

When Charlie and Vincenzo first moved to Whitney Point it was quite an adjustment from New York City. Now they're an integral part of the community and they have never regretted their move upstate.

Barstow House
Nichols, NY

The Barstow House was built by Dr. Gamaliel Barstow in 1823 in the Village of Nichols. Dr. Barstow was active in many community activities, including serving as judge, state assemblyman, senator and treasurer.

A century and a half later, Steve and Josephine Timchack discovered this beautiful building in disrepair, after it had been neglected for years. It took ten years for Steve and his sons to finally restore the house to its former elegance.

Through that time, Steve wore many hats: electrician, professional musician, collector of jazz recordings, and passionate cook. He idolized renowned chef Julia Child and learned as much as he could by watching her television shows and reading her books. With the passing of Julia, he turned to Food Network's Giada DeLaurentis for culinary inspiration.

While Steve was strengthening his culinary skills, Josephine was busy with finishing touches on the restaurant. She used the hardwood planking on the floor and a brick archway as focal points. Enhanced with antique furniture and crocheted curtains, a dining room with a warm and homey ambiance was soon created by her.

Steve often looks to his eastern European roots for recipe ideas, such as his Homemade Potato Perogi or Pork and Sauerkraut special. Meanwhile, Josephine's Italian heritage is reflected in a wide selection of pasta dishes.

The Barstow House is truly a family operation. In addition to Josephine running the dining room and Steve serving as Chef, their son Gary, his wife Tammy and their grandchildren Edward and Stephanie are part of the team and tradition.

Each dish served at the Barstow House is lovingly created by hand. Everything is homemade, including the bread and desserts. Steaks are hand-cut as needed right in the kitchen, and the chefs even grind the meat on-site. Pastas are homemade and served with Josephine's family sauce recipes. The newly-renovated second floor of the restaurant is available for small banquets and private parties, and you get the same family attention as in the dining room.

Steve likens his work in the kitchen to his days as a musician. In each instance, it's an opportunity to perform. In the old days, it was with an accordion or piano; now it's a sauté pan. But keeping his audience of satisfied customers happy is what drives him to continue striving for perfection.

4

Binghamton Club
Binghamton, NY

The Binghamton Club was established in 1880, when a charter was signed by a group of professional businessmen.

The first meetings were in rented rooms at the corner of Court and Chenango Streets. In 1923 they purchased the "Old Abbott Property" at 83 Front Street. The next year, a new structure was completed. A limestone addition was erected in 1965 to provide space for an elevator and offices.

The Club has always placed a strong emphasis on providing Members and guests with outstanding culinary experiences. In addition to serving lunch and dinner, the Club bustles with activities. Wedding receptions, business meetings and social gatherings keep the Ballroom and Banquet Rooms continually busy. Members often host private events, or sponsor an event hosted by a non-Member. Nearly forty wedding receptions were held at the Club in a recent year, many of which were "sponsored" events. Catering services are available to anyone in the community at a venue of their choice.

The Club prides itself on attracting quality staff to assure outstanding food service. General Manager Gregory McGuire has earned the "Food Management Professional" designation, Executive Chef Robert Gedman is a product of London's City & Guilds Professional Cookery Program, and Sous Chef Daniel Cusick is a graduate of the prestigious Culinary Institute of America...an all-star lineup.

While the Club offers a broad array of choices from its banquet menu, Food and Beverage Director Dianne Monico and Chefs Gedman and Cusick will work with clients to customize a menu for either in-house or catered events.

Signature entrees in the Dining Room include Steak and Ale Pie... Beef Tenderloin Tips, Shallots, Mushrooms and Guinness infused Demi Glace served in hot flaky pastry. Another popular dish is Ziti and Salmon...Ziti Pasta tossed with Shallots, Asparagus and Lobster Fume, topped with flaked poached Salmon Fillet. The Club also offers an extensive wine selection with pairing recommendations listed on the menu.

The Binghamton Club, a community institution, is still going strong after 125 years.

Broadway Diner
Endwell, NY

Steve Anastos is the kind of person who is a born leader. When he was 18, he arrived in Ottawa, Canada to take a job washing dishes. Three years later, in 1960, he owned his first restaurant. Steve wasn't afraid to take a chance, a trait he has exhibited throughout life.

His desire to come to the United States was accomplished in 1962 when he immigrated to New York City. In 1969, after working in a variety of restaurants, he joined his brothers and opened 3 Brothers Restaurant in the Bronx, just a few blocks from Yankee Stadium.Steve married and moved to Broome County to live closer to his wife's family. But the restaurant business was solidly in his blood.

He opened the Spartan Deli in 1978 and then operated a wholesale food operation. Zorba's Café on Country Club Road was his next business, opened in 1996.

Fate took a hand and Steve learned that the Boulevard Diner was available. He and his sons, Leon, John and James, huddled and came to a family decision. They would buy the diner.

It took six months to refurbish the place and give it a new name…The Broadway Diner. Why that name? Well, Steve wanted to recognize that his start in the United States restaurant business was in New York City, and he wanted to express appreciation for the New York City entertainment industry. When you walk into the Broadway Diner you'll be greeted by a delightful display of Broadway posters, NYC photos and similar memorabilia.

It wasn't easy in the beginning. Steve is fond of telling a friend that he had to cut back to working half days. What that meant to him was working only 12 of the 24 hours in a day.

Steve and his sons pride themselves on operating a true diner, just like when it was when built some 75 years ago. One could say that diners were the first fast food restaurants. You're welcome whether wearing a business suit or shorts and a t-shirt, and you'll receive fast service at moderate prices. That's what diner service is all about.

Diner customers want an interesting atmosphere, warm hospitality, old-time menu items like meatloaf or shrimp in a basket, Friday-night fish specials, a clean facility, and, most important of all, homemade offerings. Customers at the Broadway Diner receive all of the above and then some.

If you want homemade soup, homemade cheesecake, or authentic Greek cuisine, all in a relaxed atmosphere, then stop at the Broadway Diner and say hello to Steve Anastos and his sons Leon, John and James.

Brothers 2 Restaurant
Endwell, NY

Lou Masi emigrated from Italy, and like his friends Camillo and Agostino Iacovelli, he entered the restaurant business in Endicott. Lou operated Masi's Restaurant until he sold it to the Fata family in 1970.

Two brothers, Dominic and Luigi, along with their parents Giovanni and Rosina Fata, took over operations and began to build the business. They wanted a simple name that would reflect the ownership and also a name which people could easily remember, hence…Brothers 2.

Dominic and Luigi got their start in the food business working at Grover's Pig Stand in Endwell. If you order the Pork Bar-B-Q sandwich today, it's the same recipe that was originated in the early 1900's and served at the Pig Stand.

The pizza and pasta sauces are the same as Lou Masi created and came with the restaurant. Gradually, the restaurant expanded with the addition of banquet rooms in 1982 and again in 1989.

The menu has also grown. Years ago it was basically pizza and pasta. Now a wide variety of dishes, such as Shrimp Alfredo, Chicken Cacciatore and Veal Franscaise are included.

Brothers 2 Executive Chef, Lucas LaRue, may have something to do with the newer and more creative offerings. Lucas is a graduate of the famed Culinary Institute of America. He moved back home to be near his family and took over supervision of the Brothers 2 kitchen.

The banquet menu is extensive, but Chef LaRue is also open to special requests. For example, they have two wedding receptions scheduled which will be strictly vegan.

Dominic and Luigi take pride in knowing that often one of the first stops for former residents returning to the Triple Cities for a visit is often Brothers 2.

The restaurant name isn't fancy; it simply reflects what you get… two Brothers, good food and friendly service.

Bull's Head Restaurant
Binghamton, NY

Bill Erle has been involved in the restaurant business since he was 19. He began with a fast-food operation, moved to a full-service restaurant and then back to fast-food. Meanwhile, Bob Flynn opened the Bull's Head Restaurant in 1975, but by 1980, was ready to sell. Bill took over the business and has continued to serve the public exceptional food.

The Bull's Head is essentially a steak house, but they also serve a variety of chicken, seafood and Italian dishes that round out the menu.

One of their very popular dishes is called "Big Bleu Crumbles". It's a marinated sirloin steak, topped with sautéed onions and melted crumbles of Bleu Cheese. The balsamic laced marinade, enhanced with the Bleu Cheese flavor, tantalizes the palate with every bite.

Bill fills the menu with items such as Marco Polo Chicken, topped with broccoli, bacon, cheddar cheese and Hollandaise Sauce. The Linguine Imperial, with garlic butter topped with crabmeat stuffing and melted mozzarella cheese, is a winner. The Sicilian Chicken, topped with Ricotta Cheese, Red Sauce, Mozzarella Cheese, Pepperoni, and chopped sausage is always popular.

Among the specials Bill offers from time to time are Alaskan King Crab Legs…all you can eat of these delectable treats. The Early Bird Specials are unfailingly in demand with those who like an early dinner and smaller portions.

Equally renowned are the rib specials. You can choose either the Texas Beef Short Ribs with Homemade Honey Barbecue Sauce or the St. Louis Style Spicy Pork Ribs with Homemade Barbecue Sauce. They're all slow-cooked until the meet falls off the bones.

Bill and his son, Michael, have developed many of recipes, like the Bleu Cheese steak dressing and the rib rub. After taste testing various versions, they've settled on recipes that customers love.

Bill takes pride in working with the kitchen staff and always looks for an opportunity to promote from within. It isn't unusual for a young person to start out as a dishwasher and work his way up to a line cook position.

As you would expect, Bill is very particular about the steaks that he serves. After forty years in the restaurant business, he knows just what to buy and how to cut and trim the steaks to perfection.

He knows full well that, in order to succeed, you must love your restaurant and be willing to work non-stop to make it flourish. Bill Erle does love his restaurant and, after a quarter of century of hard work, the Bull's Head continues to be an area favorite.

Chestnut Inn
Oquaga Lake, NY

The Chestnut Inn at Oquaga Lake was constructed in 1928 using North American Chestnut wood. When you stroll through the Inn today, you can admire this classic wood trim throughout the building. The impressive lobby fireplace is constructed of native fieldstone.

The Inn thrived for many years, attracting local visitors as well as vacationers from the region. But, as the habits for vacationers changed, so did the fortunes of the Inn. Through the 1970's and 1980's, it closed and then opened again, then closing permanently in 1989.

Two local businessmen saw the potential of the old Inn and in 1992 they purchased and completely restored it to its original charm. The thirty guest rooms and extensive dining room took on the look of an old country Inn and it became known as Chestnut Inn at Oquaga Lake.

Now, almost fifteen years later, it was time to again give the Inn a new look. The overnight rooms have been completely refurbished and brought up to date with the latest amenities. Four suites are available that include a private bath, cable, phone and internet access. Twelve luxury suites take pampering to another level. They include whirlpool tubs, king beds and plasma screen televisions in the sitting area.

The dining area has also taken on a new look. It has been completely redecorated and new furnishing added, all complimenting the traditional look of the Inn and preserving its historic features.

A very talented and experienced hospitality professional, Larry Dunn is now in charge. Larry is a graduate of the prestigious California Culinary Academy, a Le Cordon Bleu Program. His background includes a stint at Ithaca's Boatyard Restaurant, Corporate Food Manager for the nationwide chain of The Cheesecake Factory restaurants, and, most recently, Executive Chef at Dean & DeLuca in New York City.

Larry not only brings his creative culinary techniques to the Chestnut Inn, but his sense of fashion also shows up in the new flatware, china and glasses, which are ergonomically designed to fit comfortably in your hand.

You can select from over fifty beers, such as Chimay or Otter Creek Stovepipe Porter, all of which have been selected to pair well with the new food choices that are available.

An extensive wine selection includes some hard-to-find choices like Cosentino Chardonny and Jospeh Phelps Insignia, along with popular items from Rosemont, Kendell Jackson and Rodney Strong.

Dinner at the Chestnut Inn begins with freshly-baked flatbread served with elegantly presented Eggplant Caviar, Black Olive Tapenade and Hummus. When reading the menu selections, you're tantalized with choices such as Fennel Crusted Tuna with Pink peppercorn sauce, sun-dried tomato & garlic mashed potato cupcake; Roast Duck with Strawberry-vanilla bean sauce, roasted sweet potato hash, olive herb stuffing; or Veal chop Paillard with Warm tomato-basil and garlic concasse, extra virgin olive oil, balsamic reduction, potato and onion straws.

Larry's future plans include creating his own herb and vegetable garden to assure ultimate freshness, and then, a Chef's School, catering to food enthusiasts who would like to cook like a professional chef.

The Chestnut Inn at Oquaga Lake is decades-old, but its historic past is now blended with the latest hospitality and culinary offerings.

Coffee Talk and Buffy's Burritos
Binghamton, NY

It doesn't matter much about your socio-economic status or your ethnicity, as the best conversation always seems to happen in the kitchen. Stroll into Coffee Talk, grab a cup of coffee, snack or lunch, and you'll feel like you're sitting at the kitchen table. Coffee Talk is everyone's kitchen table.

That's the way owner Mark Yonaty likes it. Even with a variety of business enterprises to keep him busy, Mark is usually at Coffee Talk to greet customers… after his morning ritual of sweeping the sidewalk in front of the shop.

Mark, like many others, cultivated his love for food in the family kitchen helping and learning from his mother. The first lesson he learned has now become his mantra, "Fresh is fresh." He's carried that lesson with him into the creation of a successful restaurant.

Mark opened Coffee Talk in 1999 for a variety of reasons. He's passionate about Binghamton and wants to do whatever he can to spark life into downtown. He planned to create an atmosphere that was not like the typical coffee shop chain. Mark and his staff have come to know their customers; often a person will approach the counter and their order will already be placed.

When the owners of another local eatery, Buffy's Burritos, decided to sell the business to focus on other enterprises, Mark acquired the name and recipes and moved it to the lower level of Coffee Talk. Chris Mollo now heads that part of the operation and prides himself on using only the best ingredients. Processed steak or chicken will never be found in Buffy's Burrito's kitchen.

Mark and his staff are constantly looking at ways to change and improve the operation. They'll soon augment the downstairs menu with burgers, steak sandwiches and fries. They're now offering a daily hot dish special along with the usual fare upstairs.

Mark is a big proponent of supporting local artists of every genre. His monthly "Featured Artist" program provides an opportunity for artists to display their work. Poetry readings are commonplace and up and coming musicians are invited to perform.

One of Mark's friends, Don Briga, recounted a story about a regular Coffee Talk customer. An elderly woman came into the shop every day and had coffee, soup and dessert. When she suddenly stopped coming in, Mark was concerned that something had happened to her. He asked around, finally found her, and expressed concern about her absence. She explained that her rent had increased and that she could no longer afford the luxury of eating at Coffee Talk. Mark insisted that she return to eating at the shop, and he and the staff would "take care of her". She's now back on a daily basis, but with one change. When she pays her check, a good portion of the money is placed in a special envelope and returned to her every month.

Yes, Coffee Talk is everyone's kitchen table.

Consol Family Kitchen
Endicott, NY

Jim and Dave Consol got their start in the restaurant business working for their uncle at Duff's…an Endicott landmark in years gone by.

In 1989, Jim decided to open his own restaurant and pattern it after Duff's, using the family recipes that had been handed down from generation to generation. He also wanted to reinforce the fact that he was offering the traditional Consol dishes that customers had enjoyed for years at Duff's. He came up with a name reflecting the Consol family recipes being used in the kitchen…Consol Family Kitchen.

You should know that family members promise not to divulge recipes to anyone outside the family. When you visit Consol Family Kitchen, you're getting the same sauce as Duff and his mother used to make. The same goes for the pizza that Duff made famous as one of Endicott's great traditions… Duff's Hot Pies…as it was called years ago. It's just as popular today, with pizza sales hitting as many as a thousand pies in a week.

One of Consol's most popular dishes is Veal Parmesan. It's so big that it's served on its own platter with side dishes in separate bowls…a magnificent feast.

Jim handed over management of the restaurant to Dave Consol and has opened a new place in North Carolina. Its name is Zio's, which is "uncle" in Italian…how fitting.

Consol Family Kitchen continues to thrive today. It's a casual atmosphere where patrons can be comfortable, wearing anything from shorts to a business suit. They provide more than ample servings of traditional Italian dishes, made using recipes handed down for generations. And you get all of that at affordable prices.

Duff Consol would be proud.

Cortese Restaurant
Binghamton, NY

It was the height of the depression and, like most Americans, the Cortese family struggled to make ends meet. It was common for kids of this era to take after-school jobs to supplement the family income, and Nate Cortese was no exception. He worked at Milasi's Café on Carroll Street, cleaning up after closing and eventually moving up to dishwasher.

After high school, Nate answered the call to duty and served in the U.S. Navy in the Pacific Theater- including surviving a killer typhoon.

When he returned home, he joined his mother, father and brother in the restaurant business. The early restaurant resembled a neighborhood bar serving complimentary pizza to its patrons.

Customers loved the pizza, or hot pie, as it was called in those days. The crust on Cortese pizza was "unique," as it still is today. The recipe was developed by Nate's mother and remains a secret shared with trusted staff only. The family soon realized that pizza was a profit center with many customers requesting "take-out". Nate would wrap the pizza in wax paper, lay it on a slab of cardboard, and out the door it would go.

Soon the restaurant was serving spaghetti with Mom's special sauce. It, too, became a big hit. The Cortese bar was emerging as a real restaurant. The menu expanded. A parking lot, an additional dining room and later another dining room were added. Today, the take-out option includes everything on the menu and accounts for a large portion of restaurant sales.

Nate is very quick to credit his wife with the support he needed to survive in the restaurant business. He spent long hours…always working when others were out enjoying themselves…usually returning home late when the kids were asleep. Nate would slip into their bedrooms to say his nightly prayers…just to see his kids.

Their son, Chris, now runs the day-to-day operation and the menu is more expansive than ever. Many of the recipes are ones created in Abruzzi and Naples and brought to America by Corrado and Angeline Cortese. You can order everything from Jimmy Cortese's Shells Vincenzo, to the ever-popular Pork Chops Milanese style, to sandwiches and subs.

No successful business, especially a restaurant, can survive without good staff. Nate is proud that his best chefs have been with the restaurant for many years, and most started out washing dishes…just like Nate.

Delgado's Cafe
Johnson City, NY

Gary Wilson was first introduced to cooking as a student in Culinary School in Las Vegas, NV. He worked at the Union Plaza Hotel on Freemont Street and then at El Cholo Café in Reno, where he learned to cook authentic Mexican food.

He relocated to Binghamton and, after a short stint in the grocery business, found his way back to chef duties. Soon his mother and sister joined him in opening the El Cholo Café in Johnson City.

The name was chosen based on his experiences in Reno. The owners assured Gary that they could grant the right to use the name El Cholo Café.

After almost twenty years in business, in 1999, he was hit with a lawsuit by a California company claiming infringement on the use of their name, El Cholo. A year-long legal battle convinced him to relent and rename the restaurant. His sister and now partner, Sherry Humphries, suggested calling it Delgado's, which, in Spanish, means "slim one", after her slender husband.

Gary spends most of his time in the kitchen, using some of the recipes he learned in Nevada and creating many of his own versions. Delgado's salsa is homemade, as are the re-fried beans, freshly cooked tortilla chips and a number of other classic dishes.

For example, he boils and grinds pinto beans, then adds his own spice mixture to create a unique flavor in his re-fried beans. His salsa comes either hot or mild and is made fresh daily. Homemade Tamales and Chile Rellenos are always a big hit, but the Fajitas and Burritos continue to be the big favorites. And don't miss trying the Albondiga or Menudo Soup, the latter made with Tripe, Hominy and Chilies. For the more conventional palate, Black Bean Soup is served daily.

Relatively new additions to the menu are Wraps, filled with chicken strips that are plain or spiced with Wing Sauce. Or, you can order the BBQ Wrap with Gary's own Delgado's BBQ Sauce. If you want hot, that's what you'll get with this popular item. It's made using five different chilies and gives a whole new meaning to hot and spicy.

Gary also created a "Pepper Kickin Dressing and Dip". It was available in local grocery stores until his bottler could no longer handle the orders. The good news is that you can still order it on a Wrap or Chicken Salad Sandwich. It's also available at the Cafe for purchase by the pint. Gary is quick to point out that most of the Delgado's menu items are flavorful, but not necessarily spicy hot.

If you're a fan of Chili Con Carne, try Gary's, made the authentic way with no beans and lots of pork and chili flavoring. It comes with either Colorado red or Verde green chilies.

What would a visit to a Mexican Restaurant be without a Margarita? Delgado's uses the same recipe that Gary learned in Nevada, but now there are flavored varieties of Tequila if you want a touch of strawberry or raspberry. Delgado's selection of Tequilas runs the gamut, many of them are sipping quality, like a good brandy. Of course, you can also find imported Mexican beers. The latest twist is Corona's lime-flavored beer, which eliminates the need to drop a wedge of lime into the bottle.

Donoli's Restaurant
Apalachin, NY

Scott Fargnoli literally grew up in the food business. When he was six-years-old he began helping out in the grocery and meat business operated by his parents, Albert and Jo Ann Fargnoli. He learned his first lessons about working hard, the importance of sound values, and the skills of working with the public.

In 1989, at the age of twenty, Scott and a partner opened Donoli's Restaurant. In choosing a name for the restaurant they combined a portion of each of their last names. He bought out his partner before opening, but Donoli's had a nice ring to it and Scott decided to keep it.

Scott also received guidance from his Uncle Louie and Cousin Louis Fargnoli, who operated Fargnoli Distributors, a food service distribution company specializing in Italian products. They, along with Grandma Fargnoli, provided Scott with some of the traditional family recipes that are still being used today.

Another big influence came just a month after opening Donoli's, when he began dating the love of his life, Linda, who is now his wife and mother of their two daughters.

In the early days, Scott spent most of his time in the kitchen fine tuning traditional recipes and creating new ones. He listened to his customers and found that there were certain items that were always a big hit, such as his Pasta Fagioli and other homemade soups. His unique Soup of the Day selections include Beans and Greens with Meatballs, Chicken Cacciatore with Meatballs, Creamy Potato and Ham, Creamy Mushroom, Cheese Tortellini with Garden Vegetables and Prime Rib Soup.

Scott found that his Prime Rib was in constant demand, so he began offering it every day, rather than just on weekends and holidays. It's so popular now it has become the restaurant's signature dish.

When the restaurant opened, it consisted of the dining room and a relatively small private room known as Donoli's Hideaway. Growing demand for banquets and private parties led Scott to expand with a 250-seat banquet room adjacent to the restaurant.

Since the restaurant is open every day of the year except Christmas Day, it takes an enormous amount of dedication on the part of the owner and his family to make it work.

Scott and Linda also operate a horse farm known as Fargnoli Farms, where they offer boarding and carriage service. A horse-drawn carriage or wagon is available for weddings, anniversaries or corporate events. More than one marriage proposal has occurred on a carriage ride, with a wedding reception in Donoli's Banquet Room at a later date. Now that's what you might call "full service".

Glenmary Inn
Owego, NY

Jane Taylor is a natural entertainer and party planner. She started a small catering business out of her home years ago and is proud to say that the first wedding reception which she catered called for serving 150 guests, which she executed flawlessly.

In the late 80's, Jane and her husband Robert, purchased the Pumpelly House near the river in Owego and converted it to a Bed and Breakfast Inn. It wasn't long before Jane added event planning and catering to innkeeper duties…the business thrived.

But a new opportunity and challenge was on the horizon. She learned that a stately mansion was slated for demolition. The building had a long and storied history, built in 1857 as a private residence for Henry D. Rice and his family. It's situated high on Glenmary Drive, with a grove of ginkgo trees in front.

In its next life, the building was converted to a hospital by local medical doctors. The promotional material at the time referred the hospital as "A Small Retreat for the Insane, the Nervous, and Drug Habitués, on the Cottage Plan. Licensed and Inspected by the State Commission in Lunacy".

In 1947, it was purchased by Pauline and Frank Michaels, and turned it into a nursing home that operated until 1976. The building stood vacant, gradually deteriorating until 1997 when Mr. Michaels decided that his only option was to demolish the building. Jane Taylor said "No" and rescued it from destruction, saying that it was a priceless gem with too much potential to become a pile of rubble.

Jane purchased and renovated the building and opened it as Glenmary Inn in 1998 with her son and daughter-in-law, Michael and Laurie Incitti, as Innkeepers.

Since then, the Inn has hosted a multitude of dinner parties, wedding ceremonies, receptions and overnight guests. She loves to entertain travelers doing business with local industries. Her guests have included many foreign business people, the Under Secretary of the Navy and several Two Star Admirals.

The Inn's three dining rooms can accommodate private parties from six to sixty. Jane still does much of the cooking, but is turning over the management of the Inn to her son Paul and additional kitchen staff.

Through the years, Jane became more and more aware of the need for trained staff in the hospitality industry. From simple tasks like cleaning a guest room, to properly setting a dining room table and serving guests, she saw the need for more formalized training.

With Paul Incitti in charge, the Glenmary Inn has now launched its latest program. A specially designed curriculum, accredited by the New York State Department of Labor Workforce Training Program, prepares students for careers in the hospitality industry. Prospective students include many who are about to enter the workforce and others who are considering a career change.

In the meantime, guests at the Glenmary Inn are treated like guests in Jane's home, which in fact they are.

Gramma Jo's
Binghamton, NY

Kristen Iacovelli comes from a long line of restaurateurs and has worked in the food business all her life. She refined her own skills as a graduate of Broome Community College's Restaurant Management curriculum.

When Kristen learned that the former Mama Lena's restaurant building in Binghamton was for sale, she and her partner, Jim Pascucci, seized the opportunity. She had long wanted to take a page from her family history and open a restaurant featuring what's known as "The Meatball Scamutz" (pronounced "ska-mootz").

Back in the 1950's, when her grandfather, Anthony Iacovelli and his wife, Connie, were traveling through the Lake George area they came across a sandwich with which they were not familiar. It was called a "grinder", or what is now called a "sub". Connie's brother operated a restaurant named Cosmo's on North Street in Endicott. He let Anthony set up card tables in front of the restaurant to sell his "grinders". They were a big hit, but Anthony was always looking for a new feature to offer his customers. With a little experimenting, he loaded meatballs, sauce made from his family recipe, and a combination of special cheeses . . . The Meatball Scamutz was born.

The sandwiches were such a smash that, in the early 1960's, he opened his own restaurant…Mr. Anthony's. In later years, Anthony's son, Jim, took over and operated Mr. Anthony's in downtown Binghamton.

Kristen learned the family recipes from her father and grandparents and knew that The Meatball Scamutz could again become a favorite. The Mama Lena property was acquired and the interior renovated. She wanted to call the restaurant Gramma Jo's, after her grandmother Josephine Milasi. Now she needed help designing a catchy logo. She contacted the folks at Broome Community College's ExCEL program, whose mission is to assist small and emerging businesses. They designed a logo featuring Gramma Jo's photo that is now seen on the sign and menus.

In addition to The Meatball Scamutz, Gramma Jo's features a variety of sandwiches and traditional Italian dishes. Soups are all homemade and the Pasta Fagioli is made daily from an old family recipe. For the kids, they offer a "ScamutzaRoni", with the same meatballs, sauce and cheeses served over ditalini.

Kristen's goal is to offer a family-friendly atmosphere where kids are welcome and the prices are affordable. Stop by and try the legendary Meatball Scamutz, which has been made the same way for three generations.

Hallo Berlin
Corbettsville, NY

When Rolf Babiel arrived in New York City from East Germany in 1980 he landed a construction job in Manhattan. On many days, lunch would be a hotdog from a street vendor and each time he ate one, Rolf would say to himself, "New York deserves better than this."

He knew that, if he offered authentic German wursts, it would be a huge success. So he spent the next year researching sources for the best wursts in the metropolitan area. He settled on three different German butcher shops to buy the ten different wursts that he wanted to serve. In 1981 he launched the first of his "New York's Wurst Restaurants".

It was a push-cart at the corner of 54th Street and 5th Avenue and called Hallo Berlin, which, as Rolf is fond of saying, brought German peasant food to 5th Avenue. He soon opened a beer garden at 44th Street and 10th Avenue, serving the same wursts, a variety of other authentic German dishes and a wide selection of imported German beers. To this day, Rolf refers to the cart as the "Baby", never forgetting where he started.

One day, as he was working the cart, a lovely Haitian woman happened by, bought a wurst and chatted a bit. They immediately hit it off and the rest is history…Bernadette is now married to Rolf.

Rolf's first challenge was teaching Bernadette to cook authentic German dishes. She was a quick study, once Rolf convinced her that Caribbean spices weren't a part of German Potato Salad.

Then a chance meeting changed the lives of Rolf and Bernadette. The owner of a restaurant known as Kiwi's, in Corbettsville, New York, met Rolf in New York City and convinced the Babiels to visit his upstate establishment. Bernadette fell in love with the area and felt that it would be a great place to raise their children.

So, in 1997, Hallo Berlin was born again in Corbettsville, New York. Rolf still operates the push-cart with his brother, and they are very proud of being named New York City's 2005 Outstanding Street Vendor…out of 10,000 competitors. Their second big moment came when Rachel Ray of Food TV Network fame interviewed Rolf for her appearance on the Oprah show.

These days, Rolf is in Corbettsville every weekend, and Bernadette runs the operation during the week. You can count on the same taste-tested wursts as those served on 5th Avenue, the same imported sauerkraut, pickles and herring and the same recipes that Rolf developed years ago. You'll find imported German beers on tap and in bottles, with a selection that will please most any palate.

Rolf observed that you don't have to be German to enjoy authentic German food. Bernadette has proven that you don't have to be German to cook authentic German food.

Rolf and Bernadette pride themselves on welcoming everyone to their restaurant to enjoy authentic recipes. They greet every customer with…"Berlin says hello"…or…"Hallo Berlin."

J. Michael's Restaurant & Lounge
Binghamton, NY

Working in industry for seventeen years, Mike Gennett learned a lot about finance and crunching numbers. He also learned that working in a large company just wasn't right for him.

He had developed an interest in cooking early in life, especially from his grandmother, Helen Gennett. Those experiences, coupled with a lot of reading and learning from Food Network chefs like Mario Batali, convinced Mike that the restaurant business was in his future.

He loves to develop his own recipes, often building on family traditions going back to his great-grandparents, who were originally from Naples.

Mike came across a vacant restaurant in downtown Binghamton that had formerly housed both Le Caveau and Le Chateauneuf Restaurant. The white stucco walls on the lower level of an office building immediately struck Mike as the perfect place to serve traditional Italian fare; a true touch of Italy.

Mike and his wife, Mary, who runs the front of the house, had their grand opening in 1997 and have since been serving their own selection of unique Italian cuisine. Mike is the classic hands-on chef. For example, he starts with veal bones to prepare his own Demi Glace. His Manicotti is made using homemade crepes and his meatballs are made with veal and pork.

One of Mike's favorite dishes is the Veal a la Mary, named for his wife, which is Sautéed Veal, Shrimp, Scallops and Mushrooms in a Mornay Sauce, with a splash of Marsala Wine.

J. Michael's also serves grilled pizza, cooked on the grates of their grill directly over an open fire. Mike believes that the idea for grilled pizza originated in Florence, Italy. The pizza crust has a slightly smoky flavor, giving it a unique taste. He offers varieties of toppings from Tomato Mozzarella, Garlic & Herb to Proscuitto, Sauteed Spinach, Tomato, Romano & Herb.

Mike is an owner-chef who believes that the owner must be on-site overseeing every aspect of the operation. To assure complete consistency, Mike personally orders all the food and beverage products, prepares all the sauces and sees that his recipes are followed precisely.

It's a labor of love for Mike. There is nothing he'd rather do than create his culinary delights. Well, maybe an occasional round of golf.

Jailhouse Restaurant
Owego, NY

Are you in Kansas City? Or Memphis? No, you're in downtown Owego at the Jailhouse Restaurant, but the ribs and Blues music will easily carry you away.

Partners Fred Gage and Dave Ferris had been promoting Blues Concerts for some time and, when the chance to acquire the Jailhouse Restaurant came up in early 2005, they seized the opportunity to combine their love of great music and awesome food.

With Fred's son, Justin, in the kitchen creating some of the best ribs this side of Kansas City and Memphis, combined with legendary Blues musicians, the restaurant has made its mark in the Southern Tier, including earning the People's Choice Award at the 2006 Roberson Annual Food Fest.

When you stroll through the restaurant you can feast your eyes on an impressive collection of posters. From the Beatles Gold Record, to the original Woodstock poster to the rare Jimmie Hendrix; the music memorabilia boggles the mind. And don't miss the poster signed by all the artists who have visited the restaurant that is posted at the entrance.

The artists who have visited the restaurant include John Lee Hooker, Jr., Hubert Sumlin, Rod Piazza and the Mighty Flyers, Tommy Castro, Roosevelt Dean, and many others.

The unique environment with customers dining in authentic jail cells adds to the mystique, but the great food is what really sells the Jailhouse Restaurant.

The restaurant has been featured on Good Morning America, a PBS Special and the Travel Channel, so it's no wonder that customers come from miles around to sample Justin's fare.

If you want authentic smoked ribs, you've come to the right place, but you can also treat yourself to pulled pork, thick-cut pork chops barbecued chicken or beef brisket. They're all slow cooked in the Justin smoker with his own special rub.

Or, if you're in the mood for Fettuccini Alfredo, Orecchiette with Chicken Breast or Ahi Tuna, the choices are almost endless. And a special that's a huge favorite is the Pork Osso Bucco…don't miss it if you have the chance.

And for lunch, some favorites are The Kingwich, named for B.B. King, which consists of egg battered chicken sautéed with tomato, artichoke hearts, and Brie cheese, served on garlic bread. Or you can try the Howling Dog BBQ Sampler, with ribs, pulled-pork and deep-fried Memphis bologna or the very popular Artichoke Spinach and Cheese Dip.

Fred and Dave both love to have a good time, but they're very serious about serving their customers great food in the most hospitable atmosphere possible. And that's just what they do.

Kampai Japanese Restaurant
Vestal, NY

Soon after Ryoichi "Richard" Matsushima arrived in New York City, he met Mr. Sato, a meeting that changed his life. Sato owned a Japanese restaurant near SoHo, where Richard was living. One day Richard was asked if he'd help out in Sato's restaurant on the weekend. Before long, he was Maitre d' and his restaurant career was launched.

He opened Kampai in Vestal in 1975 and began with Hibachi Grills, a cooking technique made popular by the Benihanna chain of restaurants. It featured Japanese chefs cooking, chatting with customers and providing entertainment, all at the same time. The chefs prepared traditional American selections like beef, chicken and seafood, but all with an Asian influence.

On the 10th Anniversary of the restaurant, Richard's introduction of Sushi to the community presented new challenges. It meant finding the right chef, arranging for shipments of the best quality fish available and importing unique products from Japan. Richard is very proud that his head Sushi chef, Takashi Kobayashi, has been with the restaurant for 20 years and still holds court at the Sushi Bar.

On his 20th Anniversary, Richard expanded the menu to include traditional Japanese entrees like Tempura, Sukiyaki, Yoki Niku, Beef Negimaki, and Beef and Chicken Teriyaki. The change meant that the restaurant had to operate three separate kitchens to accommodate each of the specialties, but it was just another challenge for Richard.

No small business survives for over thirty years without key employees. In addition to Takashi, Richard has been fortunate to have Fumiko Gamache with him for 30 years. Having employees that long is a tribute to them, but it's also a tribute to Richard.

The restaurant has expanded to include a banquet room which can accommodate up to 50 people. It is very popular for wedding rehearsal dinners and similar events.

One thing that has not changed in 31 years is Richard's insistence on quality and consistency. He continually taste-tests menu items, especially the sauces. Although he isn't a chef, he knows exactly how every dish should taste and exactly what the consistency of the Tempura batter should be. You can be assured that every entrée will taste the same each time you visit the Kampai Restaurant.

Richard's modest smile and welcoming demeanor have charmed

customers for over 30 years. Children and grandchildren of his early customers are now regulars. His simple philosophy is to listen to his customers, give them what they want, and be sure that they're happy when they leave the restaurant. It has certainly worked for Richard Matsushima.

Little Venice
Binghamton, NY

Rocco (Rocky) Carulli, with his brothers Sebastian (Sam) and Anthony, opened the Little Venice Restaurant at 242 Court Street in Binghamton in 1946. That section of Court Street was like a miniature restaurant row, with Celeste Tavern and Mary Ann's next door. They moved to 22 Chenango Street in 1961, and then to their current location at 111 Chenango Street in 1968.

Sam retired in 1974, and his nephew Romeo Lisio took over as chef and is making the famous sauce. The restaurant was run and owned by Rocco Carulli, Robert Carulli and Romeo Lisio until Rocco's death in 1984. Robert and Romeo and their wives ran Little Venice until 2002 when Robert retired. Romeo and his son Piero are the present owners and guardians of the secret sauce recipe.

They're delighted that Piero has joined them as a partner and that their daughter, Gina, can be seen in the restaurant on weekends.

Long before art galleries sprung up around downtown Binghamton, Little Venice was known for its artwork displayed throughout the restaurant. Rocky loved paintings and, whenever he saw one which he liked, he bought it and hung it in the dining room. No one is quite sure why, but, as you admire the paintings, you'll notice Rocky particularly liked those portraying monks.

The location may have changed through the years, but the recipes are the same as in the 1940's. If you look at one of the original menus, you'll see most of the same items listed today. Little Venice is famous for its red sauce, which Romeo and Piero cook in fifty-gallon batches every day. People have speculated for years about their secret sauce ingredients, whether carrots or, most often, applesauce. The Lisio family will tell you that it contains neither of them and, if you analyze the sauce and find either carrots or applesauce, they'll give you the restaurant.

They grind their own meat to make meatballs. They also make all of the soups, sauces and dressings from scratch. Pasta and pizza dough is made by hand, as are the ever-popular Ravioli and Manicotti.

You'll find a variety of pizza choices, including "Hot Pie", which has a little sauce, grated cheese and no toppings, just like it was served in 1946. They also offer White Potato Pizza and White Garlic Pizza, in addition to the more traditional pizzas topped with a large variety of meats and vegetables. The steaks are all hand-cut to order and are also available with an olive oil and garlic dressing known as Pizzaioli style.

A few years ago, a customer asked if they would ship pasta and sauce to a relative who had moved to another state. They accommodated the request and the word got out. Now they ship these items by Federal Express to every state in the country. The legendary sauce is enjoyed nationwide…and folks still speculate about the "secret ingredient".

In addition to Rocky's artwork, you'll also find autographed photos of a multitude of dignitaries who have visited the restaurant, including Phil Rizzuto, Liberace, Floyd Patterson, Jimmy Breslin and David Copperfield. When Red Buttons performed at the Masonic Temple, he had dinner every evening at Little Venice, often entertaining family, staff and customers.

Now in its third generation of family ownership, Little Venice is carrying on the traditions that the Carulli brothers started sixty years ago.

Mario's Pizza
Vestal, NY

Paul Francavilla opened Mario's Pizza in December 1970. His plan was simple: serve New York-style, thin-crust pizza baked in a brick oven, using homemade dough and sauce.

One of Paul's delivery guys was a SUNY Binghamton student, Craig Gillenwalters. Craig left the area after graduation in 1982, but returned to town a few years later, married Connie and they purchased the pizza parlor. Mario's Pizza has been under their operation since that time.

The business is located in what was previously known as the Vestal Plaza, and now known as Vestal Park. In the early days, the Plaza was bustling with shops, restaurants and a busy grocery store. Like many similar shopping plazas, things changed. The grocery store closed, followed by the other retail outlets. Craig and Connie hung on, delivering to university students and serving a loyal, local clientele who liked the New York City atmosphere, and especially the style of pizza which Mario's serves.

A local developer eventually bought the plaza and brought in two new companies, employing dozens of people. Mario's business began to brighten again. More recently, a student housing complex has been built that surrounds the pizza parlor. So Craig and Connie have expanded the size of the dining area and have added new menu items.

The good things at Mario's have not changed. Just like in 1970, the pizza dough is started by hand, hand-tossed and baked in a brick oven on a 2" stone slab, a true New York City-style pizza. In addition to pizza, Mario's subs are very popular. The unique Spiedies that Craig prepares offer a surprise. They are much hotter than those normally found around town. The pasta dishes have become favorites along with Veal, Chicken and Eggplant Parmesan.

New menu selections that came with the expansion include seafood dishes, Mussels Marinara and Shrimp Scampi. The shop is what you might call "fast casual" with restaurant quality food. Craig and Connie take supreme pride in serving both the local and student communities and keeping a local tradition alive and well.

Festa Corrado
Cortese Restaurant
Photo By Ed Aswad

Party Wurst
Hallo Berlin
Photo By Ed Aswad

Hickory Smoked Pork Osso Bucco
Jailhouse Restaurant
Photo By Ed Aswad

Three Way Filet
The Chestnut Inn
Photo By Ed Aswad

Lemon Chicken with Greek Spaghetti
Park Diner and Restaurant
Photo By Ed Aswad

Tripe in Red Sauce
Pronto Restaurant
Photo By Ed Aswad

Nellie's Famous Chocolate Cake
Our Country Hearts Restaurant
Photo By Ed Aswad

Pasta with Spinach Parmesan Pesto
Whole in the Wall Restaurant
Photo By Ed Aswad

Summer Shrimp Quartet
PS Restaurant
Photo By Ed Aswad

A Medley of Baked Treats
Wagner's Cakes and Cookies
Photo By Ed Aswad

Coquille St. Jacque
Number 5 Restaurant
Photo By Ed Aswad

Fajita Dinner
Delgado's Café
Photo By Ed Aswad

Roasted Corn, Salt Potatoes and Rib Eye Steaks
Senator Libous Annual Steak Roast
Photo By Ed Aswad

Freshly Grilled Spiedies
Spiedie Fest Annual Cooking Contest
Photo By Ed Aswad

37

*State Senator
Tom Libous
serving a steak
to one of the
3,500 patrons at
his Annual Steak
Roast*

*Assemblywoman
Donna Lupardo
with her first
place trophy at
the Democrat
Women's Club
Chili Festival*

McGirk's Irish Pub
Chenango Bridge, NY

Tom and Patti Madison had a vision; an Irish Pub that would provide good food, a pleasant atmosphere and entertainment that everyone could enjoy. When you walk into McGirk's Irish Pub you'll be greeted by a sign that says "There Are No Strangers Here, Only Friends We Haven't Met". The sentiment reflects their original vision, painted by the late Paul Packard, who created it for Tom's home.

As soon as Tom walked into the vacant space at Chenango Commons he could picture the end result. The renovation was executed on a Design/Build format by T.J. Madison Construction Co. under Tom's personal direction. He, along with talented employees, sub-contractors and local artisans, soon made the picture a reality. It has an open, homey feeling with bookshelves, family photos and Irish memorabilia that Patti gathered from garage sales, antiques shops and countless local attics. She and the wives, mothers and sisters of the construction crew put it all together to create a cozy ambiance.

With Manager Randy Kocher, and Assistant Manager, Cheryl Plahanski, overseeing day to day operations, and Chef Matt Kelly in the kitchen, the Pub has become a favorite among locals.

One of the popular menu items is McGirk's Famous Irish Stew. It's the same recipe that Grandma McGirk brought over from the "Old Country". Like many Irish dishes, it's laden with meat, potatoes, carrots and spices in a savory broth. If you order the Killarney Chicken Pot Pie, be sure to notice the shamrock on the top…a subtle reminder of the Irish heritage of the dish. Many customers come in each week to enjoy the Friday special, Fish and Chips,

What would an Irish Pub be without a variety of classic Irish beverages like Guinness, Harp and Smithwick's (often pronounced "Smidicks"); all on tap with their own separate nitrogen pouring system. Of course, you'll also find Irish Mist, Jameson, and Bushmills Irish Whiskeys at the bar.

To top off your meal, you can enjoy a Hot Nutty Irishman with your Irish Cream Bash, a delightful way to enjoy coffee and dessert.

Entertainment has always been a big part of McGirk's operation. There's a live band Thursday, Friday and Saturday nights with the music ranging from jazz, oldies, to soft rock…and, of course, Irish music. Performers like Pat Kane's West O'Clare, Donnybrook, Old Friends and the local group, The Stoutmen, have all made appearances at McGirk's.

A tradition that's been kept alive every February is the annual Great Guinness Toast Night. At 11:00 p.m., hundreds of thousands of revelers across the country will simultaneously raise a glass and offer a toast to Arthur Guinness and attempt to break the world record for the largest simultaneous toast. For a real treat, stop by on the second Saturday of the month and enjoy "Kilt Night" where you can listen to the bagpipes and enjoy a Guinness...or perhaps a Black and Tan.

McGirk's also caters to wedding showers, rehearsal dinners, anniversary celebrations and school sports awards nights in the Blarney Room, which will seat up to a hundred guests.

It's probably safe to say that Tom and Patti's vision of an Irish Pub that would provide good food, a pleasant atmosphere and fun entertainment is now a reality.

Mekong Vietnamese Restaurant
Johnson City, NY

When Tom and Rose Trung fled Vietnam in 1979, they weren't sure what the future would hold. A sponsor arranged for them to settle in the Triple Cities community. Soon, both were working at what then was the General Electric plant, but Tom wanted to do more for their six children than production work would allow.

Tom had been exposed to the restaurant business in Vietnam, where he helped his Aunt, a chef at the International Hotel and Restaurant in the Mekong Delta. Rose's mother was a professionally trained chef who cooked for high ranking U.S. military officers.

With that background and their willingness to face a challenge, Tom and Rose scraped together enough money to open the Mekong Vietnamese Restaurant in 1992. They bought used equipment at auctions and Tom did all the renovations himself.

Meanwhile, Rose was fine tuning recipes which she had learned from her mother. She knew their customers would expect the best, and that's just what she intended to provide.

The restaurant invariably receives rave reviews on the sauces, which she makes from scratch, including the House Brown Sauce, Lemongrass, Ginger and Curry Sauces.

Reflective of the history of Vietnam, it's no surprise that many of their dishes have a French influence. A good example is the Fish Stew Sautéed in Coconut Juice with Broccoli, a 100% traditional Vietnamese dish.

Other popular menu items are chicken sautéed with various vegetables, deep fried noodles with seafood or chicken, and a wide selection of vegetarian dishes.

A large number of Vietnamese are Buddhists and many are vegetarians, so vegetarian selections are creatively prepared with a number of sauce options. However, there are certain dishes for which Rose won't allow a substitute sauce, such as the Sweet and Salted Shrimp with Broccoli, which comes with Rose's unique sauce. She knows that, for this dish, another sauce would not properly enhance the flavor.

Family is the most important thing to Tom and Rose. It's why they opened the restaurant and why they worked so hard to put all six of their children through college. The lessons that the kids learned working in the restaurant after school were just as important for their education.

The Mekong Restaurant has always been a family affair and still is.

Mountain Top Grove
Binghamton, NY

Back in the 30's, Lou Kane had a dream about serving guests clams, steak sandwiches, beef and pork barbecue and, of course, cold beer. His dream also included a covered pavilion, horseshoe pits and a softball field.

In 1932 the dream became reality. He hired carpenters from the local Union Hall to build a pavilion and he worked tirelessly to prepare the grounds. That September, he opened Mountain Top Grove at the end of Hance Road, just inside the Town of Vestal line.

It was a huge success and Lou enjoyed being the host until the day he retired. Joe and John Patrick purchased the facility in 1948 continuing the traditions set by Lou until they, too, retired and turned over the reins to Rosey and Tim Dickerson in September, 1985. The Dickersons purchased a home across the road from the Grove and raised their two children, Patrick and Leigh, as much at the Grove as at home.

Even though the business is "seasonal", the work never ends. Shoveling snow from the pavilion roof to cutting trees, landscaping and planting flowers, the family is busy all year round.

Rosey and Tim live by the old adage, "If it isn't broke, don't fix it." They knew that the recipes which they inherited from the Patricks were a big hit. The popular sauce served with the grilled Rib Eye Steaks is the same as one that was used for decades. It's still made in ten-gallon batches just like Lou Kane and Joe and John Patrick prepared it.

The clams are always "Certified", pressure-washed and served raw or steamed. The clams designated for steaming are hand-counted in tens, put into mesh bags and steamed in large pots of boiling water. One of the best parts of steaming clams is the chance to capture clam broth for the Grove's famous Clam Chowder.

The seasonal staff usually numbers ten to fourteen, many of whom are teenagers. But Rosey and Tim also inherited a few long-time employees from the Patrick family, like Reggie Raynor, who has been working at the Grove for over twenty-five years. You can always find Rosey and Tim keeping a close eye on things and pitching in to help where needed.

The largest bake ever hosted had 1,999 guests, who consumed over 40,000 steamed clams. Each season about 5,800 lbs of Rib Eye Steaks are cut on site, grilled and served. That's nearly three tons of choice beef!

Speaking of records, some of the clam openers decided to have a contest to see who could open the most raw clams in the shortest time. It was a heated competition with Rosey and Tim's son, Pat, setting the record with twenty clams opened in one minute.

If you're wondering what will happen to the Grove if Rosey and Tim ever decide to retire… son Pat and his wife Sarah would love to continue maintaining the traditions that have been in place for almost seventy-five years. The Dickersons often say, "It's an area tradition not to be denied."

Nirchi's
Endicott, NY

When Rocco Nirchi was a teenager, he helped his mother, Nicolina, operate the family grocery store on the north side of Endicott. It was in an era when small grocery stores dotted the neighborhoods and customers stopped in almost daily to pick up items for the day's meals. It was also a time when workers "packed their lunch"; so, many stores had a deli and sold cold cuts for the lunch sandwiches. Nicolina also made an outstanding pizza and began baking sheets in her kitchen oven selling them by the piece at the deli counter. Soon, customers were asking to take home a sheet, and Nirchi's Pizza was born.

When Rocco took over the business, he knew that there was a tremendous potential to expand the pizza business to other areas in the community. He also realized that it was the kind of business that really needed an owner-operator. His solution was to franchise Nirchi's Pizza to those who would operate the business as he did, hands-on. The idea took off, and today there are 12 franchised Nirchi's Pizza stores in operation.

In 2001, Rocco and his wife, Patty, decided that something Endicott needed was a fine-dining restaurant. They renovated a building on Washington Avenue and opened "Nirchi's Restaurant on the Avenue". Things were off to a great start when a devastating fire struck just four months after opening. It meant starting all over again, but Rocco and Patty were committed to making this dream come true.

The restaurant can accommodate 140 in the dining room and 50 in the adjoining private room. Rocco and Patty make a great team. Rocco handles the back of the house and Patty the front. She views everyone who comes in as if they were a guest in her home and insists that the staff do the same.

The menu was developed working with their chefs, but also features some old family specialties, such as the pasta sauce, Rocco's mother's Veal and Peppers and the namesake Chicken Nicolina. They use nothing but the finest fresh ingredients and spare no cost in providing outstanding dishes. An example is the immensely popular Maryland Crab Cakes, made using only fresh lump crab meat.

Rocco is also proud of a custom-built cooler designed to dry-age steaks. The Nirchi's Signature Dry Aged Rib Eye is a huge favorite and a tribute to Rocco's innovative dry-aging technique. The menu is wide-ranging, from Cappellini with Tomato Basil Sauce to Surf-n-Turf, and everything in-between.

There are a number of secrets to Nirchi's success. One is Patty's attention to her "guests", making sure that everything they order is exactly what they expected, and then some. This is one of the reasons that they have received the Wine Spectator Award three years in a row.

Another secret is a simple one, namely hire the best possible staff. Their bartender, Chris Jakatis, is a local legend for remembering his customers and what beverage they regularly order. Two outstanding servers are Rose Nasoni and Mary "M.J." Balogh…people who are more like family than staff. It's not uncommon for customers to ask to be seated in one of their sections, knowing that the service received will be outstanding. Their manager, Michele Galbreath, has years of experience as a chef and restaurant manager.

One of Rocco and Patty's sons has followed the family path and operates a Nirchi's Pizza in Syracuse, and their other son is serving his second tour of duty in Iraq as a Navy Corpsman. Of course, both are a tremendous source of pride for their parents.

Rocco and Patty will both tell you that the restaurant business is a labor of love. Nirchi's on the Avenue is a great example of the fruits of those labors and that love.

Number 5 Restaurant
Binghamton, NY

The water was scalding hot in the twin sinks in the kitchen of the Paradise Restaurant. A Union Endicott high school senior was up to his elbows washing dishes. Paradise owner Albert "Lampy" George had introduced Jim McCoy to the restaurant business.

It was the first of many food service apprenticeships for Jim. He tended bar while at college, learned to cook at The Villa and Fountains Restaurants during summers under the tutelage of Chef Russ Rodriguez and finally worked his way up to manager for the legendary Guido Iacovelli.

After directing operations at Iacovelli's Chef Italia production plant, Jim continually kept a keen eye open for his own restaurant opportunity. It came on August 4, 1978 when he took over Number 5 Restaurant. It was a struggle in the early days as Jim rotated between cooking, hosting and tending bar. The hours were long and grueling and things weren't going as well as he'd like. However, he upgraded the menu, brought in "Oldies Bands" on the weekends and found a great new attraction in Phil Markert at the piano. Soon the place was packed.

Not content to just operate Number 5, Jim opened another Number 5 in Scranton and McCoy's Dockside on Upper Front Street. Then he established Dion's and later McCoy's Chop Shop in the then Hotel deVille. For various reasons, those restaurants are now closed. His latest venture is Lampy's Mediterranean Grill in the same location where his first mentor, Lampy George, operated.

If you wander into the kitchen at Number 5, you'll see two signs. They read "Good enough never is" and "There is no try, you do or you don't". The signs reflect Jim's business philosophy as well as his personality.

He's proud to offer a wide selection of menu items, highlighted by his signature dishes which include the Original "Greek Tenderloin, Coquille St. Jacques, Chicken Felix and Filet Mignon Oscar.

According to Jim, the four keys to operating a successful restaurant are Consistency, Quality, A Sense of Urgency and Awareness. Perhaps that's why Number 5 Restaurant has received the Wine Spectator Award of Excellence and was voted Reader's Choice "Best" Fine Dining for 15 years.

Jim is proud to publish his restaurant's mission statement right on the menu, it reads: "Our mission is to please all of you, our guests. The simplest way to do this is to provide you with the finest food, service and atmosphere possible. And the way to ensure that is to purchase only the very best foods in the marketplace, to hire and train the very best employees, and to start each day with the honest attitude that yesterday is history, and today we have to earn it all over again".

Now in his 29th year operating Number 5, Jim still thrives on the challenges of the business. From hiring and training staff to purchasing the best quality products available, Jim is the same hands-on guy that washed dishes for Lampy George 40 years ago.

Oaks Inn
Endicott, NY

It wasn't long after Richard Cerasaro's great-grandparents, Paul and Theresa Cerasaro, arrived in Endicott from Calabria, Italy, that they opened a restaurant and called it Oaks Inn. Oak Hill Avenue wasn't paved yet and it was common to see horses on the street, since much of the surrounding area was still farmland. It was 1930, and between the Depression and Prohibition, it was a tough time to be in the restaurant business. But the entire family pitched in and the restaurant thrived.

In the early days, they served a lot of pizza, then commonly known as hot pie, a term often used to attract non-Italians to a dish with which they weren't familiar. And, of course, they sold lots of pasta.

The next generation, headed by Albert "Poppy" Cerasaro, continued the restaurant traditions, and like those before him, he started his family out at a young age working in the restaurant. Poppy was succeeded by his son, Paul, who also introduced his family to the business at an early age.

His son Richard was washing dishes at 14, helping his mother and grandmother make the macaroni and sauces soon after. Richard was a natural in the kitchen, and the lessons that he learned early from his mother, grandmother, aunts and uncles were deeply ingrained.

Paul and Richard became partners, and Richard took on the responsibility for the kitchen. But, unlike his ancestors, he had an opportunity to travel and to see what else there was out in the culinary world. As often as he could, he and his friends would visit New York City and sample the wide variety of cuisine available.

In the mid 80's, Richard became the owner and chef of the restaurant. He ventured from the traditional pasta dishes through daily specials that he created. It was a great way to introduce new dishes to his customers, and he would then add the most popular ones to the regular menu.

Oaks Inn has come a long way from pizza and pasta. Richard now offers a wide selection on entrees, but some things don't change. The pasta is still homemade and the sauce is from his great-grandmother's recipe. In addition, you can select from a variety of chicken dishes, an extensive array of seafood, traditional veal dishes, and the popular selection of steaks.

Richard's veal creations have become the signature dishes of the restaurant. Topping the list is the Veal Francese, followed closely by

Veal with Artichokes and Veal Soltimbocca.

Recently, Oaks Inn was featured in Sysco Today, a magazine published by the giant food distributor. Out of nearly 400,000 customers, Oaks Inn was selected for a feature story. Quite an accomplishment!

Following the tradition set 76 years ago, there are other Cerasaro family members helping in the business. Richard's sisters Karen and Susan can be found in the dining room and his nephew Benjamin is breaking into the business.

Richard will tell you that, when you operate a family business, it becomes part of your life and that you have no choice but to continue its proud tradition; there's too much history to just let it slide. When you love what you do and you're proud of whom you are, you just make it happen. Paul and Theresa would be proud of their great-grandson and today's Oaks Inn, the area's longest operating family restaurant.

Old World Deli
Binghamton, NY

Dick Schleider and Don DeLuca opened the original Old World Deli on the Vestal Parkway in 1974. They began operating a classic deli, selling cold cuts, cheese, kosher foods, German cold cuts and fresh fish. It wasn't long before they offered subs and sandwiches due to customer demand.

They then opened branches in Binghamton, on Henry Street near the phone company and on Court Street in the area where the Embers and Home Dairy was located. Business was brisk and they opened another branch at 27 Court Street in 1982. But things began changing in downtown Binghamton. The phone company cut back on its employees, Fowlers Department Store closed and JC Penney moved to the mall. It was time to consolidate the business at 27 Court Street.

In the meantime Don DeLuca retired, but, for a while, he still dropped in to help out at the Deli. The Schleider family pitched in and all the children helped out, including Dick, Jr., who currently manages the Deli. Dick's mother, Anna Lasky, was in charge of hot entrees and ethnic foods for twenty years, until she retired. Although she's now in her 90's, her recipes are still in use.

The Old World Deli has always taken pride in its homemade dishes. Everything from the hot entrees to salads are made on premises daily. Items like the Chicken and Biscuits with homemade Buttermilk Biscuits, Macaroni and Cheese made with Real Aged Cheddar, Stuffed Meatloaf with Broccoli and Cheese and, of course, Pierogies have been a mainstay for years.

There are many secrets to the success of the Old World Deli, which has survived competition from every quarter. One is that there has always been an on-site owner. The Deli has also changed with the desires of its customers. When it became apparent that, in addition to the hot entrees, a broad selection of sandwiches was being requested, the menu expanded in that direction. More recently, entrees with a Mexican or Asian influence have been added.

Changing with the times and accommodating the tastes of the current customers is one of the secrets. When you walk into the Old World Deli, you're offered some awesome Triple Decker Sandwiches, such as The Harpur Special with Ham, Swiss, Lettuce and Tomato, or The Dick's Special with Pastrami, Swiss, Cole Slaw and Russian Dressing, or the Signature Sandwich, The Nosh. By now, you should be really hungry for any of the Triple Deckers, especially The Nosh. It's a half-pound of meat and cheese including beef, ham, turkey, cheese, lettuce and tomato.

The Old World Deli offered "fast food" before the term was invented. With its cafeteria-style service, you can be seated with your meal as fast as any more conventional fast food restaurant.

Another reason for the success of the Old World Deli is the legion of satisfied people who are catering customers. For years, a wide range of catering options has been offered, from Party Platters to Entrees such as Baked Ziti, Cranberry Stuffed Chicken and Spinach Noodle Casserole. And, if you don't have time to stop in for lunch, delivery service is also available.

As times and tastes change, The Old World Deli can be counted on to flow with the desires of its customers. In business for over thirty years…accommodating customers is the right ingredient.

Our Country Hearts
Endicott, NY

Nancy and Ed Shaw developed their own small cottage industry creating hand-painted wooden decorative pieces, which they sold from their home. In 1991, they rented a small space in a commercial log cabin at the corner of Routes 26 and 38B in the Town of Maine. The shop wasn't much bigger than the average living room and was surrounded by a variety of other small shops. A couple of years later, Ed retired from his position with IBM and joined Nancy in the business.

Customers liked what Nancy and Ed had to offer and, as some of the surrounding businesses left, Our Country Hearts gradually expanded. They found that many customers were as interested in the bookcases and other display furniture as they were in the gifts and crafts. So they expanded a bit more and offered a limited selection of furniture for sale.

Meanwhile, their son, Jason, earned dual degrees in Computer Science and Economics at Binghamton University. After a stint at a National Lab in California, in 1997 he decided that moving back to the area and joining his parents in the business made sense.

With his computer science background, Jason soon had customized programs in place for tracking sales, inventory control and accounting functions. But Jason also has a knack for sales. The gifts and collectibles part of the business had grown really well, but he saw the potential for expanding the furniture department.

Before long, Our Country Hearts had taken over almost the entire building and included a furniture department, offering virtually all American-produced products made of solid oak, maple and cherry and suitable for any room in the house.

Then, Our Country Hearts occupied the entire building with the exception of a restaurant operated by another family. Nancy, Ed and Jason huddled and decided...why not operate the restaurant too?

In late 2003, after major renovations, the restaurant opened. It has a wood ceiling with log beams, floral print wallpaper, and stained glass fixtures. All of the solid oak tables and chairs were pulled directly from the furniture inventory. The overall ambiance might be described as contemporary country.

The Our Country Hearts chef is Jeff Glosenger, and his wife, Lisa, keeps a careful eye on the dining area. Jeff worked in a number of kitchens in the area, learning from each chef with whom he worked. One chef who stands out is Manley Tuttle, who was the chef at the Music Box on Willow Street in Johnson City. Some may remember the late Glenn Gardner, who opened the Music Box as a jazz club with great table-side cooking. Chef Tuttle was one of Jeff's most influential mentors.

Jeff has added his personal touches to the Our Country Hearts menu and is always anxious to try something new with his daily specials. For example, his Haddock and Scallops are offered a variety of ways through the week, such as Tuscan Haddock, topped with spinach, feta and tomato and broiled in garlic butter, or the Casino Scallops, which are broiled with peppers, onions & bacon in a Worcestershire butter sauce.

If you like barbecue, you should try Jeff's Jack Daniels Chicken and Ribs platter. It's another of the specials that is offered from time to time. And the pies! They're all baked on premises, and the Lemon Meringue and Coconut Cream Pies are outstanding. During the summer, you might want to sample the Coconut Cake. The restaurant also offers an "Early Bird Special" each day, featuring many of the regular menu items at a reduced price.

Our Country Hearts has come a long way, from a 600 square-foot shop in 1991 to filling the entire complex today. From gifts, to furniture to Sunday morning omelets that you would die for, it's now all part of the Our Country Hearts legend.

Park Diner and Restaurant
Binghamton, NY

The Park Diner, a Southside institution since 1940, began as a classic 15-stool diner. Not so many years later, Jim and Chris Papastrat and their brother-in-law Louie Diamantakos were all working at the Red Robin Diner in Johnson City. Jim, being the oldest, was focused on learning as much about the restaurant business as possible, aware that one day he'd own his own diner.

In June, 1967, Jim had an appointment to see the Park Diner and make a purchase offer. The owner had him stop by at 10:00 p.m. and, with one light bulb burning, the place looked good. Jim and the owner made a deal then and there. Returning the next morning to see the place in full light, Jim's first thought was, "What the hell have I done?" Not to be daunted, Jim and his partner Louie, along with Chris and other family members, got to work scrubbing , painting and getting ready to open.

In the meantime, Chris set out on his own learning experience. He worked in hotel dining rooms around the country to garner the management skills which he knew would be needed when he joined his brother at the diner.

In the late 80's, Louie retired and Chris became a partner in the business. At that time the diner was open 24 hours a day, and it was customary for people of all ages to stop in for breakfast after a night out on the town.

They expanded the diner, adding additional seating areas. Things were good...until one August morning in 1999. Chris was listening to the car radio while driving to work and the broadcaster was telling the public to avoid driving on Conklin Avenue because the Park Diner was on fire. He rushed to the scene and found Jim already there and smoke engulfing the entire building.

Once the fire was extinguished, Jim and Chris surveyed the damage and immediately decided that they would rebuild the Park Diner...bigger and better than ever. They had a vision of how the new Park Diner and Restaurant would look. They wanted an open airy feeling, but with enough privacy for customers to chat. They also wanted to maximize the spectacular view of the river, downtown Binghamton, and the surrounding rolling hills.

It was also an opportunity to change and expand the menu, departing from traditional diner dishes to a broader selection of salads, seafood,

54

chicken and veal. But they kept some old standards, like serving breakfast items from the time that they open until closing, serving as many as 1800 eggs a week.

Any discussion of the Park Diner and Restaurant wouldn't be complete without talking about the fabled "Table of Knowledge". Regular customers would come in and, rather than sit at the counter, they headed to a table near the kitchen door. It became a community table, where the problems of the world were discussed…never solved…just discussed.

Jim and Chris look forward to coming to work every day, which contributes to the friendly atmosphere at the diner. They're both very quick to credit their 99-year-old mother, Mary, with being the inspiration for them to succeed in the hospitality business.

Fresh food creatively cooked and served in a social atmosphere is the recipe for success for Jim and Chris Papastrat.

Parkview Hotel
Owego, NY

Downtown Owego's Parkview Hotel has a long and storied history. It has operated under various names through the years, including: the "First Temperance Exchange House", "Old Joe DeWitt's Place", "The Page House", and "The Dugan House". It obtained its current name in the 1920's.

In 1972, Joe and Louise McTamney took over the restaurant and, while they're still actively involved, they have turned over the day-to-day management to their daughter, JoAnne McTamney Murphy. Like her parents, JoAnne doesn't hesitate to pitch in wherever necessary. From cooking their specialties to seating and serving customers, you can't miss the McTamney family touch. Granddaughters Shauna and Tara serve customers with the same personal attention that's become a family tradition. And don't miss Kelley McTamney's shrimp specials on Saturday evenings.

Walking into the Parkview you might think that you're visiting an Irish Pub. With its well-worn wooden bar, hanging Shillelaghs and overall hominess, it is like a visit to the "Old Sod". If all that doesn't convince you, take a glance at the menu. Emerald Green Salads, Shamrock Snacks and Blarney Stone Appetizers are just some of the items with Irish monikers. On St. Patrick's Day, patrons pack the place from 10:00 a.m. until 9:00 p.m., feasting on over five hundred pounds of corned beef, two hundred pounds of ham and four hundred pounds of cabbage.

St. Patrick's Day at the Parkview Hotel can be more than just Corned Beef and Cabbage. One such day the janitor at the restaurant celebrated the holiday by buying a Lotto ticket and cashed in the ticket for forty-five million dollars...this gives a whole new meaning to celebrating.

The meat served at The Parkview Hotel comes from Thompson's Grocery, just around the corner on North Avenue, and is cut fresh daily. All of the salads and soups served are homemade and many of the recipes date back for generations. The pies are also homemade and are always a huge hit. The apples are even hand-sliced to assure the perfect size. Other favorites include Pecan, Pumpkin and Strawberry Rhubarb pies.

Then there's the Friday Night Special, Louise's Fish Fry. Customers come from miles around knowing that Louise is in the kitchen assuring that the fish is fried to perfection, just like she's been doing for over thirty years.

Many customers have been regulars for years, like Paul Cavataio, who recently celebrated his 90th birthday with friends and family at the Parkview. Herbert "Hub" Brown, who just celebrated his 100th birthday and writes a monthly column for the Apalachin Community Press, is also a regular. If you stop by about 10:00 a.m. most any morning, you'll find Hub having coffee and toast, along with twenty-five or thirty of his friends.

One of the Parkview Hotel customers once said, "It's like family down here". He was right; when you walk in the door, you're made to feel like you're part of the McTamney family.

Phil's Chicken House
Endicott, NY

Uncle Sam first taught Phil Card how to cook during his stint in the U.S. Army in the late 50's. Not long after returning home, he found himself back in the kitchen, first at the Vestal Hills Country Club and later at the Chicken Inn on the Vestal Parkway. He gradually built the business, but had a longing to operate his own restaurant. His Pastor, Rev. John McGonnell, urged Phil to go out on his own and even scouted locations for him.

In 1965, with help from realtor Russ Terry, Pastor McGonnell found a great location…the same one in West Corners that Phil's Chicken House still operates. Phil's has come a long way since that first year, when he did about $75,000 in business. Last year, the restaurant grossed $2.2 million. That's a lot of chickens… Today, Phil's will serve about 3,000 whole chickens a week and on a good weekend, another 3,000. The record-setting day was a few years ago when he served 3,500 patrons at a picnic in Owego while serving another 3,000 at an event in Elmira.

Phil uses a modified version of the barbecue sauce recipe first developed by Cornell Professor Dr. Robert Baker, but is quick to remind folks that most anyone can make the sauce…the secret is in the technique…getting it to stick to the chicken.

In addition to serving patrons in the dining rooms, Phil's does a very brisk take-out business and, in the summer, you can find his chicken at picnics throughout the region.

Years ago, it was Phil in the kitchen and 4 or 5 servers working the dining room. Once the patrons were served, the staff would sit down and eat, then pitch in to hand-wash the accumulated dirty dishes.

Today, Phil is pretty much retired, having turned the operation of the restaurant to his son Kevin, who started working in the restaurant when he was ten. He has a loyal cadre of long-time employees, including three who have been with him for over 30 years.

Phil Card's greatest satisfaction has come from turning customers into friends who visit Phil's Chicken House on a regular basis.

The Plantation House
Vestal, NY

Tom Iacovelli was destined to be a restaurateur. He started out washing dishes at the Vineyard Restaurant as a teenager for his father, the legendary Guido Iacovelli. Over time, he learned to be a waiter, bartender and eventually a manager.

In addition to the Vineyard, he also worked at Coco's and later at the Vestal Steak House, where he was General Manager for sixteen years. After his father passed away and the lease ran out at the Steak House, Tom looked for another opportunity.

A historic building in Vestal, once known as Drover's Inn, was available. He was intrigued with the possibilities that the property presented. The building has been around since 1844 and had housed a variety of businesses over the years, including a few restaurants. After he, and his wife Angela, looked at it four or five times, they began to see potential in the vintage building.

Once the decision was made, it was time to begin renovations. Tom concentrated on the kitchen, utilizing his experience in helping his father open dozens of restaurants around the country. Angela concentrated on decorating the various rooms to reflect the image of the new restaurant, while preserving the historic feeling of the building.

Tom thought a lot about the concept for the new restaurant. He knew how to operate a typical Italian family restaurant like the Vineyard. He also had plenty of experience with fine dining from his years with the Vestal Steak House. His research led him to a slightly different concept. Cajun and Southern Style cuisine were becoming more popular, partially because of Food Network shows like Emeril and Paula Dean.

So Tom set about working with his chefs to create a menu that would offer many traditional dishes like Filet Mignon, Lobster Ravioli with Tomato Vodka Cream Sauce and Stuffed Flounder. But for those a bit intrigued with Cajun style cooking, they created a menu laden with items with a Louisiana twist, such as Jambalaya, Bourbon Street Nut Encrusted Salmon and Chipotle Barbecued Chops.

Tom and his team are continually creating new recipes. Some recent additions include a Spinach Boursin appetizer, Chicken Oscar and a variety of Duck Breast dishes such as Grilled Duck Breast with Raspberry Cream Sauce. Another favorite appetizer for those who love both escargot and gorgonzola cheese is a delightful combination of both.

Tom is able to accommodate banquets of various sizes, since there are a number of separate rooms in the facility. He also does off-premises catering and will work with clients to create just the right menu for a special occasion.

It's a long way from the Vineyard for Tom Iacovelli, but it's a sure bet that Guido would be proud of what Tom has accomplished at The Plantation House.

Portfolio's Café
Binghamton, NY

Portfolio's Café is a bit different from your ordinary restaurant. It's operated by Catholic Charities of Broome County. It is a program to help individuals suffering from mental illness to learn, or relearn in some cases, basic work skills. In operation since 1987, it has served over 300 clients and is still going strong.

Portfolio's started as a "co-op", selling bulk foods and soup. Sandwiches soon followed and today there's a broad array of breakfast and lunch entrees available.

Clients usually start out washing dishes and are gradually rotated through other stations like the grill and counter. Generally, they're with the program for about a year. Two supervisors serve as job coaches to both train them to do the task at hand, and also to instill a basic work ethic.

The goal of the program isn't necessarily to train food service workers, but to help clients function in the world around them. Success is measured differently for each individual. In one instance, a person found permanent employment cleaning offices. Another success story might be a person who, for the first time, was able to cook their own meals.

In addition to the regular menu items, there's always a soup-special to tempt the customers. Deliveries to downtown offices are common, along with catering services for meetings or special events. And, during the holiday season, they will sell as much as 200 pounds of their homemade Kolachky.

Manager Diane Smith takes great pride in the fact that the Café not only strives for good taste, but is also committed to serving nutritious food in a clean, attractive and pleasant setting. Seeing that someone who was washing dishes a few months ago is now gainfully employed, is the best reward of all.

Pronto Restaurant
Conklin, NY

Have you ever wondered why a popular restaurant in Conklin was named Pronto? Here's the real story. When Mario and Laura Masciarelli and Carmuele and Antionette DiLoreto were planning to open their restaurant, they gave a lot of thought to choosing the right name. The family recalled that, whenever they phoned their grandmother in Italy, she answered the phone with her standard greeting…"pronto". It just seemed right to name the restaurant using the same warm and welcoming greeting.

Everything was progressing as planned when the family was devastated as Mario passed away on June 3, 1987, just four months before the restaurant opened. They knew that they had to carry on as a tribute to this beloved member of the family.

Every business has its own philosophy, and Pronto's is reflected on the front of their menu with a special welcoming message: "In Italy a meal is not just another time of day, but a proud & cherished tradition. Our families have brought this tradition from Casacanditella to share with you. We hope the many homemade recipes become a tradition you share with your family and ours for generations to come. Buon Appetito".

Now, almost 20 years later, Antionette DiLoreto and Laura Masciarelli own and operate the restaurant, with Antionette's daughter, also named Antionette, acting as manager. Back in 1987, the restaurant was a small pizza and sandwich shop, but customer demand led to expanding both the size of the restaurant and the menu selections.

In addition to traditional homemade pastas, veal, chicken and seafood dishes, one can order the classic Italian dish, Tripe. It's interesting that Grandma Maria is the only one trusted to prepare the Tripe and its special sauce. There is no recipe; Maria knows that a pinch of this spice and a pinch of that will result in a sauce like no other.

Where else can you find the zesty, creamy tomato sauce known as Matriggiana Sauce? At Pronto's it's been popular since the restaurant opened, especially for those who like a little kick with their pasta. Garlic knots are a standard item in many Italian restaurants, but the Pronto owners claim to have been the very first in the area with this offering.

Homemade Ravioli continues to be their best seller, with the spinach filling usually outselling the cheese and chicken options. Another distinction is their Chicken Marsala, made using cubes of chicken breast, a departure from the usual whole breast.

Even though Carmuele, who is known by most as Carmen, is busy with his own business activities, he's in the restaurant most every evening chatting with old friends and making new ones.

Through the years, much as been written about the value of maintaining valued traditions. The Masciarelli and DiLoreto families not only maintain their family traditions, but they also continue to share them through their classic Italian recipes and friendly service.

PS Restaurant
Vestal, NY

Rick Dodd was the only male in home economics class at Binghamton Central and that was his first real introduction to cooking. During and after college, he tried different jobs, but always returned to his first love-the kitchen. He seemed to have a knack for cooking. After working at the Peppermill, Augostino's and Copperfield's, he found himself at McCoy's Dockside Restaurant.

The move was great for two reasons. It was an opportunity to hone his culinary skills and that's where he met his wife and business partner, Sylvana, who was also working at the restaurant.

Jim McCoy asked Rick to move down town to Number 5 as kitchen manager. It was another great opportunity to learn more, especially the management side of the business.

That experience paid off on November 13, 1990. That morning Sylvana drove to Albany to pick up their liquor license and that evening Rick served the first eight dinners at PS Restaurant - now owned by Rick and Sylvana Dodd.

Rick has sharpened his skills over the years, and in 1991, the American Culinary Federation awarded him the designation of Certified Executive Chef. PS Restaurant has also received Wine Spectator's Award of Excellence every year since 1997. Meanwhile, Sylvana manages the front of the house, assuring that the service matches the food in excellence.

Rick is innovative in the kitchen and loves to create an eclectic blend of flavors, often with an Asian fusion touch. He will often create the evenings special from scratch, based on what fresh products he has in the cooler. If Rick were a guest at PS, he'd probably order either the Roasted Duck with Chambord Raspberry Sauce or the Pan Seared Quail with Pineapple BBQ Sauce. Sylvana would start with Pan Seared Foie Gras with Ginger, Fig and Lime Butter Sauce and then move on to Veal Ian, which is stuffed with a Thai Chicken Sauté and served with a Thai Peanut Dipping Sauce.

Rick and Sylvana make an impressive team. They serve great food, give great service and, on top of that, they're nice people.

Red Robin Diner
Johnson City, NY

The Red Robin Diner has authentic, classic, Art Deco design, containing stainless steel steam tables, lots of chrome and Formica counters. It was moved from Binghamton to its current location in Johnson City in 1959. It had a 15-stool counter and 5 tables before an additional dining room was added.

The current owners, Chris and Pat Anagnostakos, have operated the Red Robin since 1970. Chris first learned to cook in his native Greece before arriving in the U.S. in 1955. His first job was cooking at a diner in Youngstown, Ohio. He then joined his uncle at a restaurant in Brooklyn. Next, he met and married Pat Papastrat who convinced him to move to her hometown – Binghamton.

Arriving in the Southern Tier, he cooked for Guido Iacovelli at The Pavilion Restaurant and then for Charlie Zades at the Fountains Pavilion, where he helped prepare meals for sell-out crowds who came to see guests such as President Gerald Ford and Senator Robert Kennedy.

His next cooking stop was the Queen Elizabeth Diner in downtown Binghamton. After three years, his lease ran out, and he and Pat bought the Red Robin Diner in 1970.

After 55 years in the restaurant business, Chris still takes pride in his homemade specialties. A day at the diner starts with peeling and boiling potatoes for home fries. His popular meatloaf and meatballs are made with the same recipe that he's used for decades and his daily soup specials are legendary among regular lunch customers. John Cenesky, an attorney with nearby offices, who has been a regular for over 25 years, describes the diner as "historical and classical…and should be visited".

Every Friday, Baked Macaroni and Cheese is the daily special, made from scratch like all of his menu items. For years, customers have come in just to sample his Chili Dogs, knowing that the sauce is homemade -- the same recipe he's used for generations.

Johnson City has gone through many changes since 1970; the shoe factories are gone, there are fewer retail shops, you can't buy a hamburger for 30 cents, but you can still find Chris and Pat Anagnostakos at the Red Robin Diner. They're classics, just like the diner.

Red's Kettle Inn
Johnson City, NY

Back in the 1920's, Anthony Sobiech, Sr. got his start peddling fruit and vegetables from Binghamton to Endicott and back. In the 1940's, he was named manager of the Polish Community Home, but work never completely interfered with his love of sports. Tony Sr. made a name for himself playing semi-pro baseball and football on championship teams.

In 1942, he took over a restaurant known as The Kettle Inn and in no time his nickname, "Red", was attached to the restaurant name.

Since the restaurant was just a few blocks from Johnson Field, it became the home-away-from-home for many Binghamton Triplet baseball players. Mrs. Sobiech was like a second mother to them, often preparing home-cooked meals just for the team. One of those young players was Whitey Ford, who was to visit the restaurant again in 1988 to renew acquaintances with his old friends. Red was also a close friend of then Triplet General Manager, Johnny Johnson, who later took on the same role for the Yankees…a fortunate relationship for the Sobiech family when it came time for tickets to Yankee games.

When Tony Jr. was growing up, his father always told him to go to college and never go into the restaurant business. Well, Tony Jr. took half the advice...for a while. After receiving a degree in mathematics from Le Moyne College, he worked for various corporations around the country, wrote computer programs, and did a stint in Los Alamos, NM analyzing x-rays of plutonium castings.

Then fate called him home. In 1973, his father's failing health demanded a family decision. His mother could no longer run the business, so Tony Jr. decided to take over the restaurant. In his younger days, he had learned to cook from his mother and the restaurant's long-time chef, Milton Pasky, so stepping into the kitchen was a natural move.

After the Triplets became history, the restaurant continued attracting sports enthusiasts. Red's Kettle Inn was a sports bar before people knew what one was.

Tony Jr. expanded the restaurant by adding a banquet room in what was once Eddie Ives' automobile repair shop. He's still in the kitchen, preparing the pizza sauce like Milton Pasky did, promoting his Friday night fish fry special and making sure that the restaurant doesn't lose its special ambience.

Sports memorabilia, including photos of his father in his baseball uniform, adorn the walls. You'll see many Yankee photos and memorabilia and if you ask, Tony may show you the dollar bill signed by Whitey Ford in 1988.

So much as changed, but so much remains the same.

Russell's Steak and Seafood House
Endicott, NY

In 1979 Bob Russell attended a private party at the Surf and Turf Restaurant and happened to strike up a conversation with the owners, Harold and Irene Feeney. He was asked if he'd like to buy a restaurant, which immediately sparked his interest. After he and his wife Sally took a closer look, they decided that it was time to take the plunge.

They took over the restaurant and gradually added more dining space to accommodate the growing business. In the late 1990's, they moved to their current location across from the EnJoie Golf Club and renamed it Russell's Steak and Seafood House.

As soon as you enter the restaurant you get the feeling that you're in a shrine to the New York Yankees. There are Yankee signs and autographed photos adorning the walls. If you happen to be a Red Sox fan, you can count on a spirited discussion with Bob's brothers Matt and Pete, who can be found tending bar. On days that the Yankees are playing, you're sure to find Matt wearing a Yankee hat or tie.

Russell's is truly a family operation. In addition to Executive Chef Bob Russell in the kitchen, Sally running the front of the house, and Matt and Pete behind the bar, you'll also find their son, Brad, who is a Penn State Restaurant Management grad, in the kitchen, joined by daughter, Patty Saxby, a Culinary Institute of America graduate and Sally's sister, Sharon Tzivanis. Jeff Russell is head chef for off-premise catering. Now that's an impressive kitchen crew!

On occasion, you'll also find Jim Tzivanis pinch hitting behind the bar and Jim Saxby as utility player. Other family members who can be found in the restaurant include Dean and Kelsey Tzivanis, Elizabeth Eraca, and Suzanne Spring.

Bob and the kitchen staff love to create their own versions of many culinary classics. For example, they use filet mignon for their famous cheese steak sandwich and they also stuff a boneless, skinless chicken breast with filet mignon that has been sautéed with chopped onions, green and red peppers, rice and seasonings and topped with a cheddar cheese sauce.

Another favorite, which was named for a long-time customer, is the Veal McNeil. It's lightly breaded veal, topped with shrimp, scallops and mushrooms in a lemon, wine and butter sauce.

Two other very popular items are Bob's prime rib soup and the pumpkin bread. Customers can take a loaf of the pumpkin bread and a container of soup home…and many do just that.

Being located close to the EnJoie Golf Course for over a quarter of a century, it's no surprise that many of the BC Open players, such as Craig Stadler, Fred Couples and Jay Haas, have frequented the restaurant and have become friends with the Russell family.

Russell's Steak and Seafood House is a comfortable family restaurant where the owners know the names of their regular customers and what they're likely to order….and even Red Sox fans are welcome.

Scott's Oquaga Lake House
Oquaga Lake, NY

"The friendliness of a bed and breakfast…the excitement of a cruise." That's how Ray Scott describes Scott's Oquaga Lake House, a family resort just a short drive from downtown Binghamton and located on pristine Oquaga Lake.

It all started in 1869 when John Hale Scott journeyed from Vermont and settled on a farm on the shores of the lake. Soon thereafter he began taking in boarders and, through the years, expanded the farm house and added guest houses to accommodate additional travelers and vacationers.

On Christmas night in 1921, the house burned to the ground. The Scott family met the challenge and the house was rebuilt by the following Memorial Day, just in time to open for the season.

Ray (who is known to his friends as Scottie) and his wife Doris and their daughter and son-in-law, Patty and Gary Holdrege now manage the resort, and the sixth generation of the Scott family is involved on a day-to-day basis.

The focus of the resort has always been on the family. The activities offered are mind boggling. Free golf on two nine-hole courses, waterskiing, bowling, tennis, canoeing, volleyball, sailing, softball, bocce… and the list goes on.

Entertainment continues to be a big attraction. After dinner each evening, guests are treated to a show. It's often a well-known performer like Steve Pass, the Sgro Brothers, Will Stafford, David Black or Claus Evans. The Scott Family Revue is a popular show. All family members perform their own song and dance routines.

Another favored activity is dancing. Binghamton's talented ballroom dancer, Chuck Williamson, is often on hand to provide lessons. If ballroom dancing isn't your choice, you'll find line dancing, folk dancing and square dancing. If you happen to know Scottie, it will come as no surprise that he calls the square dances.

The resort is situated on 1,100 acres and has 125 guest rooms, all with private baths. It operates on a Full American Plan. In addition to all three meals being provided, all of the activities, including golf, are included in the package price.

Meals are served in the main dining room and guests select from a variety of menu items that change daily. Typically, the dinner menu will include an appetizer, soup, salad bar, a choice of five entrées and dessert bar.

The well-equipped and spacious kitchen is perfect for serving a large number of meals quickly and efficiently.

Twice a week, guests are treated to a ride to the Scott's Mountain Top Pavilion for a picnic lunch. Of course, live music and entertainment are part of the lunch.

If you live in the area or will be passing through, you owe it to yourself to make a stop at Scott's Oquaga Lake House…like two families do who have been vacationing at Scott's for the past 70 years.

Many people don't realize that the resort dining room is open to the general public. The Scott family welcomes everyone to join them in the dining room. Just call and make a reservation.

Scottie, Doris, Patty and Gary, and the other members of the family stand ready to make your visit a memorable one…a family tradition since 1869.

Sharkey's
Binghamton, NY

In 1947 Peter and Victoria Sharak bought a restaurant on Glenwood Avenue and renamed it Sharkey's, which happened to be Peter's nickname. Little did they know that, years later, Sharkey's would be featured in such publications as Bon Appetit, Gourmet, Money Magazine, Roadfood, The Washington Post and The New York Times. Few businesses can make such a claim.

Since the day that they opened Sharkey's has been famous for two menu items, Steamed Clams and Spiedies. In the late 40's, they sold three dozen clams for $1.00 and had a line of customers waiting to get in. The price is a bit more these days, but their Tuesday and Thursday Clam Night Specials still pack in the crowds.

Sharkey's Spiedies have become legendary. Peter and his sister-in-law Marie Sharak still use the Spiedie marinade recipe that Peter Sr. developed 60 years ago. And, while the Spiedie Fest Cooking Contest hasn't always included a restaurant division, Sharkey's came in first every time that they had the opportunity to participate.

While being interviewed, Partners Peter and Marie took care of a customer who was picking up a 40-pound order of Spiedie meat to take to New Jersey for a celebration of her father's birthday. The customer went on to say that her four brothers, who live in New York City and weekend on Lake Ontario, stop for Spiedie meat on every trip. That's the kind of dedication you find with Sharkey's customers.

Over time, the menu has expanded to include a variety of seafood items, including Scallops, Shrimp and Smelt, a very popular SPOC (Sausage, Peppers, Onions & Cheese), City Chicken, and ethnic favorites like Kielbasa, Holupki and Pierogi.

Binghamton University students have been regulars at Sharkey's since the time that the university was known as Harpur College. In fact, they recently had an eight-foot banner made, welcoming Harpur College grads back for a reunion.

When asked what Sharkey's has done differently than some other business which haven't survived as long, Peter's reply was simple, "What did we do different? We didn't do anything different."

And he's right. The layout is the same, the booths have been there for over 60 years, the bowling game is still popular and, of course, the Spiedies and clams are the legendary recipes for success at Sharkey's.

The Silo Restaurant
Greene, NY

As a kid, Gary Kurz loved to be in the kitchen with his mother, helping and learning. In high school he enrolled in the home economics class and claims to this day that it wasn't to meet girls.

His parents purchased what was formerly known as Ye Olde Silo, simplified the name to The Silo, and began building a reputation for excellence. With Mae in the kitchen, Stanley behind the bar, and son Gary waiting on tables, it was a true family operation.

In those days, the road wasn't paved and patrons would sometimes arrive on horseback or snowmobile to have dinner and watch the phenomenal sunsets from the Silo vantage point.

It wasn't all work for Gary. One day that stands out for him is January 11, 1975, the day on which he met Joanne, his future wife.

When his parents passed on in the early 80's, Gary took over the operation, mastering skills in the kitchen with Chef Doug Mack, who has logged thirty years with the restaurant.

In 1985, a fire threatened to destroy Gary's vision of what the restaurant could become. An incredible show of community spirit prevailed as friends and customers pitched in to clean up the fire debris in record time.

He has since added a banquet room and extensively landscaped the grounds to enhance the natural beauty of this unique setting.

Gary loves to dig into one of the Silo's twenty-ounce porterhouse steaks, a baked potato laden with sour cream and butter, with Brussels sprouts on the side. Gary knows how to cook and obviously knows how to eat as well!

Many customers come for the great food, others for the unique atmosphere and view of the rolling hills. Still others may come to be greeted by Gary in his own inimitable and sometimes irreverent manner.

South Side Yanni's
Binghamton, NY

When brothers Dino and George Kermidas decided to open their own restaurant over eight years ago, they named it in honor of their father, John. South Side Johnnie's it would be, until a friend reminded them that most of John's friends called him Yanni, the Greek version of John. So the name became South Side Yanni's…perfect. The name honored their father and also recognized the Kermidas family heritage…a family that has been a fixture on the south side of Binghamton for years. Opening a restaurant in another part of town would be unthinkable.

The southeast corner of South Washington Street and Vestal Avenue had been home to some raucous nightclubs, so, when they took over the space, the first challenge was to let people know that the atmosphere had changed and there was now a family restaurant on the corner.

Dino and George put together their business plan. They'd offer affordable dinner specials every day, an assortment of Greek dishes, an assortment of items from the grill, entrees like Shrimp Scampi and Grilled Swordfish and a kids menu. They executed the plan and now, eight years later, it still works. When you work at Yanni's it's like being part of an extended family. Chef Rick Cullen has been on board since the first day, as have servers Kim Foody and Sue Whalen. They all treat their customers as part of the family.

Chef Cullen prides himself on the homemade soups he creates each day, but the most popular item on the menu is the Wednesday night special, Chicken & Biscuits with real mashed potatoes.

A devastating fire next door at the Art Theatre closed the restaurant for two and half months. After scrubbing, painting and more scrubbing, Yanni's re-opened with all of the original staff back in place.

The regular customers are what keep the restaurant going. Dino and George often greet the same families every week or two. The restaurant guarantee is friendly and efficient service and good food at affordable prices…that's South Side Yanni's.

Spiedie and Rib Pit
Binghamton, NY

In the early 1950's, John and Sam Lupo, Sr. operated a grocery store and meat market at the corner of Watson Boulevard and Rogers Avenue on the north side of Endicott.

The Spiedies sold in the store were in such demand that, in 1963, they opened Lupo's Char-Pit in Endwell to accommodate the growing orders for this legendary treat. After John passed away, his widow Ruth bought Sam's share of the business and she and her family continued its operation. Her daughter Susan and her husband John Schofield were both working at the Char-Pit when they decided to branch out with their own shop.

In 1993, they opened the Spiedie and Rib Pit on Upper Front Street in Binghamton, using the Spiedie marinade developed by her family years before.

John and Susie, in a departure from tradition, decided to create their own line of Specialty Spiedies to attract a wider range of customers. With trademarked names like Buffalo Style, Endwell Style, Caesar Chicken, Spiedissimo and Greek Style, the innovative line took off. As to be expected, one can purchase bottles of marinade and Buffalo Sauce at their store.

Spiedie and Rib Pit is consistently ranked high in the Press & Sun-Bulletin "Reader's Choice Awards", coming out on top for the past two years, which makes John and Susie quite proud.

Catering off-site events has also become a large part of their business. With portable grills and fryers, they're able to accommodate hundreds of hungry patrons.

The hospitality business is their blood. Susie grew up in the business and John's father worked at landmarks like the Arlington, Sheraton and Frederick hotels. Today, John's sisters, Mary Grace and Taleen work at the restaurant. And, John and Susie's daughter Katelin, an accomplished actress, appeared in the television reality show "The Restaurant".

John and Susie also offer franchise opportunities to those who would like their own Spiedie and Rib Pit, like the one which Susie's sister Elizabeth operates on the Vestal Parkway.

Susie and another sister, Marie Lupo Lawton, have now embarked on a new food adventure. They've installed ovens in the upper level of the building and are busy baking a variety of cookies and other treats under the name "Sugar Mama's Bakery".

Only time will tell what new ideas will spring from the minds of John and Susie. The community anxiously waits for whatever is next.

The Cellar Restaurant
Owego, NY

The Cellar Restaurant has been in business since 1982, but it sprang to life when Bob and Sandy Layman took over in 2003. They turned it into what many area residents believe is Owego's fine dining restaurant.

Sandy keeps an eye on the front of the house, while Bob's culinary creativity works wonders in the kitchen. He brings years of experience as a chef at Coco's, Drovers, the Owego Treadway and the Chestnut Inn to The Cellar. But it's his knack for creating his own sauces and spice combinations that brings customers back.

Bob makes everything from scratch, from the Béchamel Sauce served with Eggplant Lasagna, to the Dried Cherry Sauce on the Hazelnut Crusted Duck, to the fourteen homemade salad dressings.

Bob and Sandy decided to replace the conventional appetizer selection with their personalized Grand Tasting Menu. It's a Tapas-like selection of gourmet treats that can be ordered either as an appetizer or in combination as an entrée.

The Grand Tasting Menu includes items such as Grilled Marinated Ahi Tuna with Wasabi Cream & Ginger Cilantro on a Jasmine Coconut Rice Cake, Pan Seared Sea Scallops with wilted Spinach on a bed of Jalapeno Cream and Duck Confit with Plum Sauce, braised Daikon Radish & Hearts of Palm Slaw.

The Cellar sponsors a quarterly wine dinner, featuring Bob's most creative offerings carefully paired with appropriate wines. If you try the Sunday Brunch you must sample Bob's version of Eggs Benedict. It's a Lobster Hash, topped with wilted Spinach, Filet Migon, a Poached Egg and Hollandaise Sauce.

The Cellar also caters to special events and periodically hosts an evening with psychic Phil Jordan. You'll find entertainment such as Curt Osgood on hammered dulcimer and other local favorites. A glance at the Guest Book will find patrons from all around the area and as far away as Montana, Texas, Florida, California and even Italy.

Bob and Sandy offer an extensive wine selection and a number of specialty drinks such as the Key Lime Martini and the Ultimate Manhattan.

If you want the ambiance of a magnificent Susquehanna River view, try lunch on the Cellar porch. Pair the view with a specialty croissant sandwich and tasty home made bagel chips or soup, and you may not want to return to work.

Evenings are like having a dinner party every night at the Cellar Restaurant, and the best part is that Bob will do the cooking….day and night.

The Sherwood Inn
Greene, NY

The site of the Sherwood Inn in the Village of Greene has been the location for various Inns since 1803. The Sherwood Inn, as it's known today, was built in 1913 by Mrs. J.J. Blodgett in memory of her father, John H. Sherwood. The grand opening of the Inn was May 1, 1913. It operated under various owners until a disastrous fire in 1962.

In 1979, a well-known building contractor, Ed McGowan, purchased the property and did a complete restoration. Not long after, he sold the property to an operator who let the building fall into disrepair. It was put up for sale at a foreclosure auction.

The bad news was really good news for John and Tricia Lien, who were tiring of wrestling with bureaucratic jobs and were longing to open a Bed and Breakfast or Country Inn. They had been looking for the right opportunity for about three years when they learned of the availability of The Sherwood Inn.

Along with Tricia's parents, Pat and Delores Fragola, they ventured into the "Country Inn" business in 1995. Pat brought his business acumen and accounting skills, Delores brought her family recipes, and John and Tricia brought their enthusiasm and desire to own their own business.

After working with some highly-trained chefs, John decided to trade in his bartending duties for a stint in the kitchen. Between his mother-in-law's recipes and what he learned from other chefs, he was soon The Sherwood Inn Executive Chef. He already had a comfort level in the kitchen learned from his mother, Betty. Her ability to create a dish from whatever was available in the refrigerator and pantry, usually referred to as "Betty's Special", has often come in handy.

John is committed to making everything from scratch and to order, including his sauces for a variety of Chicken Wing flavors and Mozzarella Sticks. John refers to his Wings as "impressive", using his own blend of sauces. You never know what's next; a recent addition was Ranch Style Potato Nachos and he's experimenting with some new and different Wing flavors.

Family recipes are a hallmark at the Sherwood Inn. The Veal Cutlet Delores and Chicken Sherwood come from Delores Fragola's recipe collection. Her special touches are found in the Marinara Sauce and many others.

One of the most popular features of the Sherwood Inn is the Murder

Mystery Dinners, hosted by Chief Inspector Dwight Kemper of Scotland Yard. The show goes on at least once a month, all personally written by Inspector Kemper. The evening includes a choice of five delicious dinners, the Murder Mystery Show and a prize for the one winner who solves the mystery.

Sadly, Pat Fragola recently passed away, but the rest of the family has carried on, maintaining traditions befitting a country inn that's almost a century old.

Theo's Southern Style Cuisine
Johnson City, NY

Fifty years ago, Theo and Barbara Felton decided to leave Cordele, GA and join Theo's sister in Binghamton, NY. Not long after arriving, they settled in Endicott where they raised eight children. Since Theo and Barbara both love to cook, it was an obvious choice to end up in the restaurant business.

In 1991, they opened Theo's Southern Style Cuisine in Johnson City and have been delighting their customers with a wide selection of classic southern dishes ever since.

Their recipes come from both sides of the family, along with those they've created or modified themselves. For example, the Sweet Potato Pie, that Barbara made famous, took years for her to perfect…and perfect it is!

In addition to being good-tasting, the food at Theo's is good for you. Collard Greens are rich in vitamins, calcium and fiber and okra is low calorie, fat and cholesterol free and also rich in vitamins. Okra is served as a side dish, but it's also used as a thickener in Chicken or Shrimp Gumbo, another Theo's specialty. And don't forget the Black-eyed Peas and Red Beans & Rice, both loaded with fiber and prepared with old-time southern recipes.

Of course, the Coleslaw and Potato Salad are homemade using old family recipes just as you would expect.

Another classic is the cornbread, which is served with every meal. It's so popular that customers buy it by the sheet to take home…usually with a succulent slab of barbecued ribs or award-winning chicken.

Theo and Barbara use local products whenever they can. The ribs have come from Butcher Boys Meat Market for years, and the honey that Theo uses in his Sweet & Sassy Sauce is from Howland's Honey in Berkshire.

Theo's has been a family affair since they opened. Through the years, all the Felton children have been a part of the business. Selina, Fred, Milton, Ted, Duane and Kurt have all have done their part to grow the business and still pitch in as needed, even though they have other occupations. Tressa is now the full-time manager and Linda takes care of the business aspects of the operation; even the grandchildren can be seen helping out.

Barbara is retired…sort of. Even though she's not in the restaurant every day, she still bakes the Sweet Potato Pies and Theo tends the barbecue pit and makes the sauces. When they do have any free time you can find them tending the flower and vegetable gardens at their Endicott home.

Family has always been the top priority for Theo and Barbara. The slogan on the menu is: "Family, Faith and Fifty Gallon Drum". This is the foundation that they have built on and the special ingredient that binds the Felton family together.

Their personal values have been instilled in their children and in the business. Barbara will tell you that you must give the best you can give, be a delightful person, and treat everyone the way you want to be treated! It works well in business and has certainly worked for Barbara and Theo. She is quick to point out that their number one secret recipe for success that they love to share is prayer and the value of spiritual inner help.

Another one of Theo's slogans is: "A Taste of the South in Your Mouth". If you like authentic southern cuisine, you'll love a visit to Theo's where you'll be treated to a taste of the real South.

Tom & Marty's Town House Restaurant
Binghamton, NY

When Bill Mantas was a student at East Junior High School, a friend tagged him with the nickname "Greek" and it's stuck ever since. In fact, many of his customers at Tom & Marty's don't even know that he has a first name, so he'll always be known as "Greek".

"Greek's" father, Thomas Mantas, and his partner, Martin Mohr, opened a restaurant in 1946. It was located across the street from the current location and was known as the Town House Restaurant. When they moved across the street to make way for a parking ramp, it was logical to call it Tom & Marty's Town House Restaurant.

"Greek", like most children of restaurateurs, grew up in the business. After high school, he went to Florida State for a degree in hotel and restaurant management. Then he landed a job with a prestigious New York City restaurant, the Rainbow Room. Degree and all, he started out as Night Steward supervising about 20 dishwashers for ten to twelve hours. As "Greek" would put it, "It's the worse job that ever could be." Before long, he was promoted to a day job and things got measurably better.

Then it was a stint in the Navy and, in the late 70's, it was back to help his father at Tom & Marty's. One of the big changes in the business was when Jim Matthews brought the Broome Dusters Hockey Team to town. Suddenly, there was a crush of patrons before and after the games. It carried over after the season ended, with fans remembering the good times and great food.

Whenever you operate an establishment like Tom & Marty's, you're apt to attract an interesting character or two. Folks tend to come in, have lunch or dinner, perhaps a beverage, and create a dialogue.

Probably heading the list of "characters" would be Ward Wilson. Ward was a stockbroker, but wasn't quite your typical broker. He's the one who invented Tom & Marty's signature lunch dish, the "Boog-A-Loo", which is now known as "The Bomb". It was also at Tom & Marty's that Ward and a few of his cohorts came up with the concept for a "Yegatta Regatta", a river-vehicle race to raise funds for charity. Hence, the moniker "Admiral Wilson", which sticks to the man to this day.

To celebrate the Christmas season every year since 1946, Tom & Marty's has served "Tom & Jerry's", sometimes referred to as a hot toddy, but made with the special house recipe. Tom & Marty's has changed a lot over the years. It has moved, been remodeled twice, adjusted its menu to suit the times, but it continues to be a downtown fixture.

80

Tom's Texas Hots
Binghamton, NY

To say that Tom Martinos is adventuresome might be the understatement of the year. His career in the restaurant business is quite different than most.

Before he passed away, Tom's father, Ernie, had worked at the El Paso restaurant, which was owned by Tom's two Godfathers, Andy Papastrat and John Nichols. While working there, Ernie had developed his own recipe for a special sauce for authentic Texas Hots. Unfortunately, Ernie died when Tom was just seventeen, but he had told Tom that the recipe for the sauce was locked in a safe in his home. When Tom went to open it he found out that no one knew the combination for the safe. A call to Bennedum's Locksmiths took care of that problem. Ernie had also taken another precaution to assure the secrecy of the recipe. He had written down all but one ingredient, which he told his wife, Lois, to remember. Finally, with the help of his mother, Tom could put all the pieces together for the original El Paso Texas Hots sauce.

Tom had been a cook at the Park Diner and gained vast knowledge at the side of his Uncle Pete Sousouris and "Uncle" Louie Diamantakos. But, he kept thinking about the recipe which he had inherited and dreamed about opening his own business selling Texas Hots.

In 1980, he heard about a bus then on the market. It was a former transit bus that operated in Watertown, NY, Gettysburg, PA and finally in Broome County. Once its transit life was over, it was acquired by radio station WAAL, and used by sales manager Tom Shiptinko for promotion purpose. The radio station sold it to Rogers Trucking just before Tom had a chance to bid on it. He approached "Babe" Rogers, who was intrigued by Tom's ideas and told him to take the bus and pay him when he could.

At first, Tom called it the "Magic Bus" and transported local music fans to concerts around upstate New York, but in the back of his mind there was the haunting need to sell hot dogs. He parked the bus at the home of his sister, Jody Emmons, and began a transformation from bus to "diner". The renovations were designed and completed by his brother-in-law, Bill Emmons. Tom's a good cook, but not much of a mechanic, so Nick DeOrio became chief mechanic.

Tom's first venture with the newly renovated bus/restaurant was in 1984 when he set up shop on the Vestal Parkway, just east of the Vestal Plaza. The first day didn't bode well. His gross revenue was $7.00, and he and Nancy learned that operating without a rest room just wasn't a good idea.

Then someone told him that Dick's Sporting Goods, at that time a one-store operation on Upper Court Street, was having a tent sale. Tom approached the late Dick Stack and pitched him on setting up the bus in the parking lot to sell Texas Hots to customers. Dick, always ready to help someone start a business, happily agreed. Five years later, the bus was still in the parking lot.

But Tom, and his then wife and partner Nancy, knew that they couldn't survive operating in just the warm seasons. The next step was opening Tom's Diner a few blocks down the street. The Diner was a great success with a broad menu of breakfast, lunch and dinner offerings. However, customers kept telling Tom that they missed the bus and wanted to see the old menu with hot dogs and burgers.

So, in 2006, Tom opened Tom's Famous Texas Hots in the Kost Plaza on Upper Front Street. A painting of the original bus adorns the wall and the menu is the same as on the bus, featuring Texas Hots with Ernie's secret sauce.

Along the way, Tom added to his adventures, like the time he agreed to cater a "biker rally". It was a 24-hour gig, serving hot dogs to 800 hungry, partying bikers. At another point, he worked the Bluegrass Festival at Kellystone Park and the Strawberry Festival in Owego.

One year, a customer, who came by to take some Hots to the folks at Woodbourne Court, suggested that Tom bring the bus to the housing complex as a treat for the senior citizens living there. Before he knew it, he was there once a week for the entire season.

Tom had a lot of help along the way. When he first approached the Broome County Health Department for a Permit, Tom, who can speak more words in a minute than most people can in ten, pitched the idea to Food Inspector Pierson Orr. Pierson listened patiently, and then tossed Tom the two-inch-thick Food Service Manual and said, "Read this and come back and see me." Tom read it, revisited Pierson and found his guidance to be invaluable.

When he first set up shop at Dick's, Tom wanted to paint his logo on the side of the bus, but didn't have the money to do it. He approached the management at Pepsi, who were just a block down the street. They agreed to paint the bus as long as the Pepsi logo was included. Tom has been a loyal Pepsi customer ever since. Dominic DeLousia and Joe Tokas owned Tri-City Springs right next door and they offered the use of their garage for Tom to do the paint job. Little did they know that the next morning their tools and inventory of springs would have a coating of blue paint from the over-spray.

At first, Tom didn't even know how many hot dogs were packed in a case. A visit to Ed Menhennent at Darling's Meat straightened that out. Tom's hot dog of choice was Surgerdale's and, again, it's the only brand he buys to this day.

Similarly, he started out using Felix Roma hard rolls and that's just what you'll still find at his restaurants. His loyalty to those who helped him get started is remarkable, but Tom would just say, "It's the right thing to do".

One of his more interesting adventures was an incentive to register people to vote. The last time that Tom had voted was when he was 18 and on his way to Vietnam. But, as he heard the political debates at the bus, he started thinking that he should register again and so should a lot of other people. He decided that everyone who came by and registered to vote would get a free hot dog and Pepsi.

People stopped by in throngs. Then the bureaucrats stepped in. It seems that it's illegal to "pay" someone to register to vote and Tom's hot dog and Pepsi was considered a payment to register. Never a person to be daunted on one of his adventures, Tom then offered a free hot dog to everyone who came in, regardless of whether they registered or not. It cost him a lot of money, but hundreds of new voters were ready to go to the polls that fall.

Tom's stylish long hair now has a touch of gray, his son Michael is learning the business after school, and Nancy is back helping at the Front Street location.

Tom and Nancy will be eternally grateful to Dick Stack, who let them stay in the parking lot even after learning that Tom was bootlegging his electricity.

Most important of all, Ernie's sauce still reigns as king.

Tony's Italian Grill
Endicott, NY

In 1968, Tony Cataldo arrived in Brooklyn from his native Italy. He was seventeen when he landed his first job washing dishes in a pizzeria, but was soon making deliveries on his bicycle, and then learning the art of tossing pizza dough.

In 1973, while returning from their honeymoon, he and his wife, Biagia, took the long way home. Instead of going directly back to Brooklyn, they ventured up Route 81 and then east on Route 17. Tony and Biagia fell in love with the rolling hills of the Southern Tier and knew it should become their home.

In 1974 he and Biagia opened their first pizzeria in the Park Manor Plaza, and then in 1977, he launched Tony's in the Endicott Plaza. Their gross receipts the day they opened was $24, which left Tony and Biagia wondering what they had gotten into. But Tony had a marketing idea…two slices and a soda for $1 for school kids at lunch only. The kids flocked in and were soon followed by their parents, and once they had a taste of Tony's pizza and pasta they became regulars.

It was seven days a week for Tony and Biagia, so it wasn't uncommon to find their two young children, Giuseppe and Kathy, playing in the restaurant. After twenty-seven years at the Endicott Plaza, plans to demolish the building forced him to move to his current location on Main Street. Along the way, Tony and his brother Nick opened Tony's Café next to the river in Owego, which soon became as popular as the original version.

When it came time to design the new Main Street restaurant, Biagia took charge of the dining areas and created a warm and homey atmosphere, while Tony concentrated on the kitchen, and his pride and joy, the state-of-the-art pizza oven that's designed just like the ones that have been used for decades in Italy.

Tony's pizza has been recognized time and time again with the Reader's Choice "Best Pizza" Award. The pizza is hand-tossed and topped with Tony's own sauce.

When it comes to the restaurant's recipes, many are those created by Biagia, who is a gourmet cook. And Tony's red sauce and salad dressings are well guarded secrets; so secret that Tony is only one who knows the ingredients. But someday it will be revealed; it's buried in the Time Capsule beneath the Endicott-Johnson Arch in Endicott! Other classics include their homemade Gnocchi and Pappardelle dishes, both created from family recipes from years ago.

Along with Tony and Biagia, their daughter, Kathy Cataldo-Medionte and her husband, Vincent are active in the business. But, all seventy employees are looked upon as an extended family.

When Tony describes the restaurant business, he borrows from the phrase "There's no business like show business." For Tony, there's no business like the restaurant business. After a busy day, with the staff functioning like clockwork, and customers leaving happy, Tony will say "it's like magic".

Uncle Tony's
Binghamton, NY

Albert Nocciolino and Tony Basti took their own routes, but ended up partners as owners of Uncle Tony's in downtown Binghamton. Albert tended bar and worked in various restaurants while in college. Tony began his career as a teenager working in local restaurants. One of his claims to fame is that while he was working as a busboy at the Holiday Inn on Upper Court Street, he met entertainer Tony Bennett and his wife, who were in town to visit their son at Camp Sertoma. Later, Tony Basti traveled with Pat Monforte and Vic Fontaine all around the country.

He returned home and opened a private bottle club, then became part owner of The Carlton, a popular downtown nightspot. Meanwhile, Albert was busy building his Broadway Theater League business. Albert and Tony often talked about opening their own establishment and, when the discussions became serious, Tony started scouting for a location. He came across a vacant space on State Street formerly occupied by the Harris Army Navy store. They leased and renovated the space and opened Uncle Tony's in 1983.

The original plan hammered out by the partners is still working today. They knew that there would be potential for three different sets of customers, and they wanted to cater to each. In order to attract lunch customers, they decided to offer a hot daily special and introduced one of the area's first half-pound burgers. The soups would be made from scratch, and Pasta Fagioli and Chili would be available every day.

There was just one more ingredient to this winning recipe, and his name is John Noce. John has run the kitchen from the day Uncle Tony's opened and is still in charge. Both Albert and Tony credit much of their success to John's cooking skills.

If you like sports, want to watch sports, or just talk sports, Uncle Tony's the place to be. There are overflow crowds on game nights, and players from the Senators and Mets often frequent the restaurant.

In 1987, Albert devised a unique way to celebrate his twin daughters' first birthday. The time was just before Christmas and Albert thought a real sleigh ride would be fun. He arranged for a pair of Clydesdale horses and a wagon resembling a sleigh to give rides around downtown Binghamton. The twins loved it, as did Uncle Tony's patrons, who were also treated to a ride. It's now become a tradition. Every December, Albert and Tony arrange for the horses to show up in front of the restaurant on the Saturday before Christmas to provide rides through downtown Binghamton.

Since Albert is as busy as ever with Broadway Theater League business, Tony has become the face of Uncle Tony's. The restaurant was named for him in recognition of his popularity with downtown club patrons. Both partners feel strongly that, for a small business like Uncle Tony's to succeed, having an owner-operator on site is a big plus. Tony Basti fills that role to a "T".

The plan which the partners developed almost 25 years ago is still in place. It worked in the '80's, it worked in the '90's, and is working today.

Whole in the Wall Restaurant
Binghamton, NY

When you walk up to the counter at the Whole In The Wall Restaurant one of the first things you see is a huge scrapbook which chronicles the history of the establishment. Leila Swenson spent untold hours compiling the information. What follows is a short summary of her work.

Eliot Fiks started cooking as a child, learning from his Viennese mother and grandmother. Soon after completing his studies at Binghamton University he launched his first business, baking and selling natural whole wheat bagels. However, Eliot had a bigger dream. He was set on opening a natural foods restaurant. A lack of financial capital was more than made up for with his unlimited energy and enthusiasm. Some might even say his stubbornness exceeded those qualities.

It took Eliot three years to completely renovate a building, learning how to do it as he forged along. The big day came on December 6, 1980 with a formal grand opening of his restaurant on Valentine's Day 1981…a fitting choice to celebrate a love affair between a man and his dream.

Eliot had no formal restaurant or culinary training, but he knew that by serving food that was good for you and good tasting, he would succeed.

The restaurant clientele is as eclectic as the dining room, menu and, yes even the owner. Walk into the Whole In The Wall and you'll find young, old, students, business people and everyone in-between. All enjoying Eliot's original recipes and often listening to the pianist toiling away on an ancient piano Eliot bought for $35…his very first purchase for the restaurant.

How many restaurant owners do you know that have received a National Humanitarian Award? Eliot Fiks has. He's been recognized as an unsung hero who has affected his community in a positive and valuable way with his "Stone Soup". Like the classic children's story by that name, Eliot makes his own version of Stone Soup and donates the finished product to a soup kitchen.

The process is simple, Eliot and his staff save every little bit of unused vegetables left over during prep time, then they freeze them and when the supply builds up he turns it into soup. The vegetables, along with a little barley, macaroni, herbs and spices simmer into a delicious soup to be enjoyed to some of the less fortunate members of the community.

In 1990 Eliot was fortunate to have Stacey Gould join the organization as junior partner. Stacey brought her own brand of enthusiasm along with a management degree from Binghamton University.

Soon after her arrival they coupled Eliot's knack for making great pesto sauce with Stacey's idea of packaging and marketing the product. Today you can find it in markets all across the country, as was noted in a recent feature in USA Today.

A quarter century later, his hair still in a pony tail, Eliot Fiks continues to live his dream.

Other Food Related Businesses

Apple Hills

Behlog & Son

Butcher Boys Meat Market

Consilvio's

DiRienzo Brothers Bakery

Felix Roma Bakery

Giant Markets

Hand of Man and River Rose Café

Health Beat Natural Foods and Deli

Helen Battisti

Jim Roma's Bakery

Kathye Arrington

Lupo's

Maines Paper & Food Service

Pam Gray

Pat Mitchell's Ice Cream

Rob Salamida

Southern Tier Chef's Association

Southern Tier Specialties

SUNY Delhi Culinary Program

Tom's Coffee, Cards & Gifts

Wagner's Cakes & Cookies

Apple Hills
Johnson City, NY

How often do you see a business that has continually operated since 1848? On top of that, the business is a family farm! The Green family has operated the farm for all of those years, starting as a dairy farm and later branching out with apple trees and then a variety of other fruits, strawberries, raspberries, blueberries and cherries.

There are about 20,000 apple trees, 30,000 blueberry bushes and acres of strawberry plants. Originally, the business focus was on the wholesale distribution of apples with a storage facility that held 32,000 bushels.

Time brings change and, just as the Green family evolved from operating a dairy farm into the fruit business, they have reinvented themselves into the premier "U-Pick" facility in the area. As the number of consumers increased, it was prudent to offer food and beverages, so they opened The Apple Dumpling Café, along with a small store. It was another way to follow the example set by earlier generations. Grandma Green had always fed the farm workers and fed them well.

The Café offers breakfast and lunch with homemade soups and sandwiches as lunch specialties. It should come as no surprise that the most popular dessert item is Apple Dumplings.

The farm has been in the U-Pick business so long that grandparents bring their grandchildren to help pick and to hear stories about how it was done 50 years ago.

The view from the farm is spectacular. Located at the top of Brooks Road, it overlooks the valley in each direction. If you look directly west from the highest point, the Broome County Airport is visible at the same level. At mid-May every year, the farm celebrates Apple Blossom Day. The hills are full of apple blossoms which are so intense that they look like a field of popcorn.

The changes in farming techniques never end. The old apple trees have gradually been replaced with dwarf trees that don't exceed 15 feet in height, making for easier picking. The extensive irrigation system is fed by two ponds and modeled after the systems used in Israel to irrigate the desert. The work is eternal. If you thought winter would be a time for the family to get away to enjoy an extended vacation, you'd be wrong. Every single tree and bush must be hand-pruned every year.

Those aren't the only changes. Apple Hills sponsors an annual Easter Egg Hunt and has converted a portion of the warehouse for the pre-teen egg hunt in a room with black walls, fluorescent graphics and black light.

There's also a learning center, where school kids are taught the basics about growing crops, from seeds to store. A current expansion is adding a meeting and banquet room to the Café. The new area will accommodate tour buses and special events like birthday parties, meetings, weddings and showers.

Apple Hills, formerly known as Green Brothers Apple Hills, is now operated by the fourth and fifth generations of the Green family. Brothers Norman and Glenn, and Norman's daughter Joy and her husband Dave, now share ownership responsibilities.

It's clear that for five generations the Green family has had the ability to adapt to the times, and it's equally certain that the changes aren't over. Things that will remain, however, are the Apple Hills' emphasis on quality, the spectacular view and the feeling that you're part of the Green family. Joy is fond of saying that the family is just a steward of God's land. And they have been fine stewards for over 150 years.

Behlog & Son Produce
Conklin, NY

Behlog & Son has come a long way. It began with a small fruit stand at the corner of Louisa Street and Broad Avenue on Binghamton's East Side, growing to a state-of-the-art warehouse in Broome Corporate Park. It progressed from selling fresh fruits and vegetables to retail customers to delivering tons of produce, meat and other food related products.

Founder Sam Behlog's vision was to build a business with his son Peter who began his career as a 12-year-old helping his father unload trucks after school and during summer vacations. He worked hard, learned from his father, and soon they were partners.

The company outgrew its first location and moved to Upper Court Street. It wasn't long before that space was cramped and they moved again...to Route 11 in Kirkwood. The company prospered, continued to expand, and the time came for one more move, to their present location in the Broome Corporate Park. The new building contains 125,000 square feet of space for coolers, freezers and dry storage.

Now, along with fresh produce, Behlog & Son provides the food-service industry with a wide variety of products from steaks to salsa to spices and everything in between. Twenty-five refrigerated trucks make 250 deliveries daily.

Pete's hands-on approach to business has paid off. He completely designed the layout for the new warehouse and keeps a close eye on the quality of products that go out the door every day.

His business philosophy is simple...work hard, keep focused on moving ahead, disperse problems as they arise and surround yourself with good employees.

Pete's mother, Renee, has been an integral part of the business since the beginning and continues to maintain an office at the new facility. Sam passed away before the opening of the new warehouse, but he would certainly be proud of where his son has taken the business.

Butcher Boys Meat Market
Endicott, NY

The razor-sharp Forschner boning knife glides through the seventy-pound slab of beef like a hot knife through butter. John Fargnoli, like his father Sam, his uncle Lou and his grandfather John before him, knows just how to cut and trim a steak to perfection.

For seventy years, the Fargnoli family's meat market has been a fixture on the north side of Endicott. For thirty-five of those years, John has been part of the business. At first, he was learning the art of cutting meat. Then he trained new employees, and now he runs the market.

Learning the art of meat-cutting doesn't happen overnight. A new employee may learn the basics in a few months, but it takes years to earn John's recognition as a master meat-cutter.

When the business began, John's grandfather made his own Spiedies. He'd marinate chunks of left-over lamb, and unlike Spiedies as most of us know them, included bones in the meat. Today, John still sells Spiedies using his grandfather's recipes, but no more bones. He now sells a dry spice mixture for making your own Spiedie marinade by adding the liquids only.

Of course, Butcher Boys also makes their own Italian sausage. If you're adventuresome, they'll sell you the meat and a packet of sausage seasoning so that you can make your own.

In addition to the cuts of beef, pork, lamb, veal and poultry that you'd expect in a butcher shop, John does a brisk business selling rabbit meat. In parts of Italy, rabbit is a very popular food. It's understandable that many area residents buy it to help celebrate their Italian heritage.

John Fargnoli and his staff take pride in providing their customers with perfectly-trimmed meat of the highest quality and freshness. When you walk up to the meat counter, the person serving you is the same person cutting meat in the back room. Your questions will always be answered by a meat expert, just like when John's grandfather, father and uncle ran the market.

Consilvio's
Endicott, NY

When she was growing up, Annette Consol Schrader always seemed to be in the kitchen helping her mother and grandmother prepare family meals. Her Uncle Adolph, better known as Duff, and his mother, fostered her interest in food.

Later, she joined her brother Jim in operating Consol Family Kitchen, where they patterned the restaurant after Duff's Restaurant, keeping the family secrets intact.

But Annette had another dream. Why not bottle and sell the traditional pasta sauce from her grandmother's original recipe? The more she thought about it the more she was convinced that the idea would work. So, in 1996 she eased out of the restaurant and began renovating a building, buying equipment and supplies, and getting ready to bottle the family sauce. A year later, she was up and running with two stoves, stainless steel pots, bottles and labels. The business grew and she graduated to a 20-gallon steam-jacket cooker, and now it's an 80-gallon model.

She knew that her sauce had to be different and better than those mass-produced by giant corporations. First, she uses only fresh garlic and onions. The tomatoes which she selected after testing many options are her standard, and she won't deviate even if another brand is less expensive. Perhaps most important of all, her sauces are "small kettle cooked" and hand stirred…just like her grandmother did at home. The company slogan is, "We're sure you'll taste the difference" and, when you taste Consilvio's, you'll know why they chose that slogan.

She also needed a name for her sauce and it seemed right to call it "Consilvio's"…the Consol family name in Italy.

Today, Annette markets four sauces: Traditional Pasta Sauce from Grandma's original recipe, Vegetarian Pasta Sauce with the same hearty flavor as the traditional sauce without the meat, Marinara Sauce with lots of garlic and chunky tomatoes in the classic marinara style, and Spicy Marinara Sauce which she describes as a "forte" variation of the classic recipe.

You can now find Consilvio's Pasta Sauce in grocery stores throughout New York, New Jersey and Pennsylvania…and the market is growing all the time.

It took lots of perseverance to survive a decade competing against giant corporations. It also took a legendary family recipe, but the secret ingredient in Consilvio's Pasta Sauce is love. That's something that the big guys just can't bottle.

There's good news for the future. The Consol family culinary genes are still at work. Annette's daughter, Olivia, is very much at home in the kitchen and cooks for the family every chance she gets.

It looks like Consilvio's Pasta Sauce may be around for a long while.

DiRienzo Brothers Bakery
Binghamton, NY

The year was 1904, the Italian immigrant was Gaetano DiRienzo, and the business was a bakery located on Henry Street in Binghamton. The bakery moved to this location in 1936 and, a century later, DiRienzo Brothers Bakery is still going strong.

In the 20's, two cousins, Felice and Felice DiRienzo (yes, both were named Felice) took over the business. One of the Felice cousins had four sons, Luigi, Felice, Carmen and Anthony who bought the bakery in 1965. Eldest son Luigi (Lou) has passed away and Phil has retired, leaving Carmen and Anthony to run the business. They all grew up in the bakery, pitching in to help from the time that they were in grade school. The obligation to help the family was so strong that the boys forsook high school sports to fulfill their commitment to the business.

Over the years, the bakery expanded and the brick oven was replaced with more modern versions. No longer are bags of flour unloaded from a truck; it's now pumped from a tank truck into a 50,000 pound hopper. But the recipe that Gaetano developed at the turn of the century is still the basis for today's bread.

In the early 80's, the brothers decided to diversify by adding a deli. Luigi had an idea...let's buy a rotisserie and sell barbecued chicken. It was a great plan, but the vendor didn't send the rotisserie; instead, a deep fryer was shipped. So they decided to sell fried fish. The haddock that they buy is caught and immediately flash-frozen, guaranteeing that, when purchased by customers, the fish will be as fresh as the day it swam in the Atlantic. Their fried fish is now a local legend. Every Friday throughout the year, plus Wednesdays during Lent and Christmas Eve, the line is out the door. The breading, of course, is made with DiRienzo bread crumbs and their secret blend of herbs and spices.

The signature advertising for the bakery is a truck lofted high above the parking lot; another of Luigi's marketing ideas. It has become a local landmark, and they've even had radio personalities broadcast from the cab of the truck.

Today, Carmen runs the bakery operation and Anthony takes orders and makes sales calls. The highlight of Anthony's week is taking care of fish customers on Fridays. As he put it, it's a chance to say hello to loyal customers. He and the staff fry as much as a thousand pounds of fish on a Lenten Friday. Anthony and his wife, Rose, make a great team. Among her many talents, Rose bakes an outstanding holiday treat, Kolachki. She makes hundreds of pounds every year and it always sells out.

It's rare that a business survives for over a century, and even more rare that its success transcends three generations. DiRienzo Brothers Bakery has broken all the rules.

A fitting tribute to Gaetano DiRienzo.

Felix Roma Bakery
Endicott, NY

Felix and Carl Roma were partners in a bakery on Oak Hill Avenue on the north side of Endicott in the early 40's. In 1948, Felix struck out on his own and opened Felix Roma Bakery. Felix and his wife, Esther, ran the operation, and Felix was always quick to acknowledge that Esther made the best bread of anyone in the family.

When the business was new, bread was sold at a retail counter at the bakery and delivered both house-to-house and to stores and restaurants. In addition to bread and rolls, the bakery also made cookies, Danish and other pastries…even wedding cakes.

When Gene Roma was a kid, he started out cleaning pans, then loading and unloading the ovens. As a practical matter, he knew that if he wanted to see his parents, he had to see them at the bakery, which was their life.

As a teenager, Gene moved on to helping his father with deliveries and gradually became more involved in the business. The bakery was growing as deliveries extended to nearby communities. Gene saw the potential for further growth and urged his father to expand the bakery. In 1969, he saw his dream come to fruition. They bought property on North Page Avenue and built the bakery that still serves them today.

Along the way, home deliveries ended, pastries were eliminated and the bakery now concentrates on bread and rolls.

Some of the loyal Felix Roma restaurant customers were moving to other areas of the country and wanted to continue serving the bread and rolls that helped make them successful. Gene's solution was simple. If a customer was too far away for delivery of fresh bread, why not provide them with a frozen product. That way they could have the best of all worlds...Felix Roma bread and rolls baked fresh, regardless of where the customers were located… almost anywhere on the East Coast.

In addition to the popular products found in local markets, such as Italian Sliced bread (the favorite of many Spiedie aficionados), Kaiser Rolls, Steak Rolls, Rye, Marble Rye, Onion Rolls and Dinner Rolls, Felix Roma produces a host of other products for restaurants, stores, hospitals, universities and large institutional facilities. A product line of 99 different breads and rolls, from Whole Wheat to Multi-Grain Rolls to Ciabatta Bread, and almost everything in between, keeps all customers satisfied.

Sons Gene, Jr. and Michael are now in charge, but Gene Sr. frequently stops by the bakery to lend some friendly advice, just as Felix did for him.

Giant Markets
Broome County, NY

Giant Markets have been a community institution since 1933 when they opened the first self-service supermarket in New York State. It was a revolutionary idea. For the very first time customers were using wicker baskets and selecting products from shelves without the assistance of store clerks. But that was just the beginning. Giant Markets newest concepts were on display at the 1939 New York World's Fair. Not bad for a young company from Binghamton, New York.

Since then, they have grown and expanded, but have always been a leader in providing outstanding customer service, a hallmark of Giant Markets for over seventy years. The business has been continually modernizing, from departmentalized cash registers to electronic scanning… from wireless shelf labeling systems to state-of-the-art energy saving systems. All twelve stores offer banking and financial service, utility payments, money orders and myriad other services.

When browsing the aisles of any Giant Market, you'll notice a wide selection of products from local companies like Crowley Foods, DiRienzo Brothers Bakery, Felix Roma Bakery, Genegantslet Maple Products, Kutiks's Honey, Lupo's, Nirchi's Pizza, Pat Mitchell's Ice Cream, Salamida's, Spaulding Bakery, Theo's, and Whole in the Wall. It's just another way that Giant Markets supports the local economy.

What's really unique is the commitment to our community. "Working together, we can make our community the very best it can be." isn't just a slogan to Giant Markets; it's a way of life for the business. "Round-Up for Chow" raises thousands of dollars for the Chow food pantry. The "Shop For Charity" program is an opportunity for non-profit organizations to generate revenue by distributing redeemable vouchers. And who hasn't walked into a Giant Market to be greeted by someone from a neighborhood organization selling baked goods, candy bars or tickets to a fundraising event?

The company also supports a variety of community activities. Giant Markets helps sponsor events and organizations such as the Spiedie Fest and Balloon Rally, Tri-Cities Opera, Binghamton University, Broome Community College, Binghamton Philharmonic…the list goes on and on.

Giant Markets… a local institution and a good neighbor.

Hand of Man and River Rose Café
Owego, NY

Thirty years ago, at the urging of another downtown business owner, Pat Hansen purchased a commercial building on Front Street in Owego. In those days, the buildings situated along the river had fallen into some disrepair, but Pat and her husband, Roger, were committed to helping restore downtown to its previous luster.

Hand of Man started out with booths rented to various vendors, but Pat's giftware and collectibles soon took over the entire first floor, and soon after the second floor as well. And, if you happen to be in the mood to shop for decorative Christmas items all year long, you'll find them at Hand of Man.

Along with a wide variety of gifts, collectibles and ornaments, you'll find a selection of seasonal candies, coffees and teas, jams and jellies, salsas, relishes and sauces, along with a line of Sea Fare Premium Crabmeat.

Tucked away inside the Hand of Man is the River Rose Café, operated under the watchful eye of Chef Becky Blair. Becky has a real knack for creating unique homemade soups, wraps, sandwiches and salads. Of course, Becky's superb desserts always attract customers.

During the summer, lunch is also served on the deck overlooking the Susquehanna River. With the abundance of flowers and decorations, it's often referred to as "Owego's Little Riviera".

In keeping with the ambience created throughout the store, the River Rose Café features an English High Tea five times a year. Guests are pampered with a three-course luncheon featuring a pot of tea, and such treats as quiches, scones and fancy desserts. Of course we can't tell you about the surprise ending to the luncheon…then it wouldn't be a surprise!

The Teas will accommodate thirty at each of two sittings and have become a "must do" event for patrons from all around the Southern Tier.

Downtown Owego has changed a lot in the past thirty years, but Pat, Roger and their daughter, Jackie Biller, have met their goal of making Owego a nicer place to live, work and shop.

Health Beat Natural Foods and Deli
Johnson City, NY

For many years, Michele Moelder just didn't feel well. From her childhood years until her 20's, she suffered with colds, pneumonia and mononucleosis. She began changing her lifestyle, eating healthier and selectively using vitamins and minerals. For the first time she began enjoying good health.

The logical next step for Michele was to open a health food store, which she did in 1983. As things progressed, it made sense to formalize her interest in nutrition. After three long years, she became a Certified Nutritionist. She now considers the education aspect of her business as important as selling natural food products and nutritional supplements.

She didn't have room in the first store for produce and meats, but, after moving to her current location in Johnson City, she expanded her inventory to include a wide variety of those products.

In addition to counseling individuals on nutritional issues, Michele conducts cooking classes at her store to show how a person can balance meals with protein, whole grain, vegetables and dessert.

Some of her favorite meals include Red Lentil Vegetable Soup, Oriental Baked Tofu with Brown Rice, and Whole Grain Blueberry Muffins. You can find these recipes, along with many more, in her Health Beat Natural Foods Cookbook.

Personally, Michele is a pesco vegetarian, which means she eats fish but no meat. Her customers include vegans, vegetarians and those who simply want healthy natural foods.

She also caters to those who are afflicted with Celiac Disease by stocking a variety of gluten-free products and by sponsoring a support group to discuss ways to make lives healthier.

Michele doesn't just sell a healthy lifestyle, she lives it.

Helen Battisti
Binghamton, NY

This mother of three grown sons has completed two marathons, but she's not done running yet. Her long-range goal is to complete a marathon when she's eighty! And, if you know Helen Battisti you, (or your children) should be watching the newspapers for the story of this accomplishment in the years to come.

Helen isn't just a wife, mother and marathon runner. She's also a highly-respected Registered Dietician and Nutritionist. Through her formal education, research and practice, she understands the complexities that surround what most of us view as a simple daily routine – eating.

It's hard to pick up a newspaper or watch television news without seeing a story about childhood obesity or the increase of Type II Diabetes in the over-forty population.

Despite the weight-loss industry grossing over 50 billion dollars in revenue every year, with 45% of the female population and 25% of the male population on diets at any given moment, 66% of American adults are overweight or obese, and 15% of our children are seriously overweight. The sad fact is that "diets" have a 95% failure rate.

You have to ask…why? The answer isn't simple, but if you look at our culture and how our eating habits have changed over the years, it may be understandable.

It isn't just super-sizing; it's the overall size of the portions that we've become accustomed to. If you do a Web search for "Portion Distortion", you find a site that shows how our portion sizes have changed over the years. We used to eat a bagel with 140 calories; today's larger bagel will treat you to 350 calories. Another example is a typical blueberry muffin. Twenty years ago it was worth 210 calories; now it's a whopping 500 calories. Also, remember that eating one extra snack on a regular basis piles on the pounds. A "little" 250 calorie snack a day can add up to a ten pound weight gain over a year.

And it isn't just the size of our portions; it's also what we eat and when we eat it. Too many people skip breakfast, eat a light lunch and then have a heavy dinner. Remember the old adage that breakfast is like a king, lunch is like a prince, but supper is like a pauper. You don't need an abundance of calories to sleep!

Helen also has some advice for those who take vitamins and supplements. First, be sure to tell your physician exactly what you're taking to be sure that there's no negative interaction with any of your prescribed medications. Second, especially if you're taking a number of supplements, make an appointment with a Registered Dietician to help to see the "big picture". Your vitamins, supplements and daily diet may, in fact, be more than your body can tolerate. You're probably familiar with the Recommended Daily Allowances (RDA), but did you know that there is also an Upper Tolerable Limit? Be sure that your daily meets the Recommended Daily Allowance, and is less than the Upper Tolerable Limit.

In her book, <u>Tomorrow's Weigh…The No-Diet Way to Lose Weight</u>, Helen outlines a comprehensive approach to better health. "You will feel wonderful – about yourself, about your body, about your food, your sleep, your confident personality, and your exercise program."

With a sensible approach to what you eat and how you exercise, who knows, you may be joining Helen at her next marathon run.

Jim Roma's Bakery
Endicott, NY

The name of the horse was Angelina. The driver was Carl Roma. The employer was Battaglini Bakery. The job was delivering bread house-to-house. That was Carl Roma's start in the bakery business.

In 1941, Carl, having learned the baking business from the bottom up, opened his own bakery at 110 Oak Hill Avenue, Endicott, with his partner and cousin, Felix Roma.

In 1948, Felix left the partnership to start his own bakery, and Carl soon brought his son Jim into the business, moved to their current location in 1954.

Long before the retail store and deli were added, retail customers would come to the bakery for bread, rolls or pizza. There wasn't even a counter, just a table and an antique cash register, but it worked.

In 1964, Jim made a fateful decision. He knew that, to continue to grow and prosper, the business needed to change tactics, so he built an addition on the bakery and opened a retail store and deli. It was an instant success.

The bakery business isn't easy. Many weeks meant working 80 hours or more. Jim is quick to say that a little luck doesn't hurt either.

For years, Jim Roma's Bakery has been delivering "hot bread' to retail outlets on Sunday mornings. If you haven't experienced a loaf of Italian bread, bagged as it comes out of the oven, still warm and aromatic... then you haven't lived.

And if you attend the Festival of St. Anthony and try the fried dough or grilled pizza...you should know that the dough came from Jim Roma's Bakery...as much as 3,250 pounds in a good year.

Jim Sr. recently passed away and his sons, Carl and Jim, Jr. run the operation. Prior to his passing, Jim, Sr. always enjoyed popping in, having a cup of soup and looking things over.

Over the years, Jim Roma and his family have always helped those in need by supporting many community causes. Endicott has been good to the Roma family, and they have been good to Endicott.

A winning combination!

Kathye Edwina Arrington
Owego, NY

Kathye Arrington takes the importance of preserving one's heritage very seriously and does a lot more than just talk about it. An accomplished artist, Kathye teaches workshops on African Mud Cloth painting, Banana Leaf Art, Eskimo Art and Japanese Paper Dipping.

Her dedication to promoting multiculturalism goes beyond the fine arts. Kathye is able to blend her artistic talents with an interest in authentic West African cooking. Using carefully researched recipes and her artistic presentations, Kathye brings the fine arts to the dining room.

There were a number of family recipes that Kathye was familiar with and enjoyed as she was growing up. But she wanted to dig a little deeper and began researching other recipes as a way to link back to her heritage. She knew that African slaves in America used ingredients and recipes from their native land as a way of to preserve a little of their culture.

Research yielded a number of such recipes, and a visit to her father's family in Mississippi was quite revealing. Recipes similar to those that her research yielded were being used by her grandparents and had been handed down through the years.

Kathye is now doing her part to keep the preservation of her culture alive by sharing the recipes and techniques that date back hundreds of years.

Some of the dishes that she creates include Akaros, from Nigeria. It's made with black-eyed peas and served with a special dipping sauce. Another is Kulikuli from Mali…a peanut biscuit that can be baked or fried. From Ghana comes Avocado with Groundnut Dressing. It's a delightful combination of avocados and peanuts.

Her Chicken and Groundnut Sauce may be served with rice, millet or potatoes. A favorite as Kwanza is being celebrated is Benne Cakes, another West African dish. Benne means sesame seeds, which are eaten for good luck.

Recipes for these classic West African dishes are included in the recipe section. When you try them you'll taste a bit of history.

Lupo's
Endicott, NY

Steve and Sam Lupo, Jr. got their start in the food business working for their father, Sam, Sr., and their uncle John Lupo. They owned a grocery store and meat market at the corner of Watson Boulevard and Rogers Avenue on the north side of Endicott.

The Spiedies sold in the store were so popular that in 1963 they opened Lupo's Char-Pit in Endwell to accommodate the growing demand for this celebrated treat. After John passed away, his widow Ruth bought Sam's share of the Char-Pit, and Sam went on to open similar restaurants, including the S&S Char-Pit in Binghamton – named for "Sam and Sons".

But the handwriting was on the wall for small independent grocers. Competition was fierce and Sam knew that he had to do something different and do it quickly. Since competing with big corporate businesses was just about impossible, why not sell a product to them instead of competing?

Lupo's had some great family recipes for Spiedies and Italian Sausage that had been developed in the early 1950's. They packaged the meat and Giant Markets agreed to sell the special meats. Customers loved the products and the new enterprise took off. They already were bottling the Original Spiedie marinade, but knew that there was a market for others. Sam Sr. personally developed the Lupo's 50th Anniversary Italian Supreme Marinade to commemorate that milestone. Now there are eight marinades and sauces for almost any kind of meat, fish or vegetable.

The wholesale operation now services stores from the Hudson Valley to Corning and from Albany to Wilkes Barre, spreading the Lupo name across the northeast.

Since the company has never used preservatives, they were constantly looking for other ways to extend the shelf life of their products. Sam came across a new concept called Modified Atmospheric Packaging. It removes some of the oxygen from the package and doubles the shelf life. Customers can be assured of freshness when they purchase a Lupo's product.

In addition to the original Spiedies and Italian sausage, the company now offers chicken sausage, marinated pork chops and pork barbecue, marinated chicken breasts, and a variety of stir fry dishes.

The S&S Char-Pit is thriving and they'll grill the Spiedies that you purchase at no extra cost, a great offer, especially in the winter when you're craving a summer time Spiedie.

The company takes a lot of pride in participating in a wide range of community events. From the Danielle 5K Run/Walk to the BC Open and the Spiedie Fest Balloon Rally, they try to serve as many events as possible.

Lupo's also decided to take on the big guys, like Hormel and Hillshire Farms in a pork competition. Lupo's Pork Stir Fry won first prize!

One of their proudest moments was when they received a Citation from the 3rd Brigade Team of the 2nd Infantry Division for Outstanding Support. Lupo's provided enough Spiedie Marinade for our brave men and women serving in Iraq to have their own "Spiedie Fest", a well deserved proud moment for the company.

Sam Jr. and Steve had two lessons drilled into their minds at an early age...summed up with two words – quality and service. Those lessons have served the company well for 55 years.

Maines Paper & Food Service
Conklin, NY

How does a small distributor of candy and paper products emerge two generations later as one of the country's leading independent food-service distributors with annual revenues exceeding $1.95 billion?

It takes hard work, perseverance and talent, all of which Floyd, Bill and David Maines have demonstrated to be part of the family gene pool. Second generation owner, Floyd Maines, started the expansion, and, when sons Bill and David joined the firm, business mushroomed.

A giant part of the company's growth has come from servicing large chain restaurants, both casual dining and fast food. It's an enormous challenge to meet the needs of those establishments, but Maines Paper & Food Service exceeds all expectations.

Corporate Headquarters and a huge distribution center are located in Conklin, NY. They also have ten additional distribution facilities servicing thirty-five states. Obviously, coast-to-coast distribution is not far down the road.

Maines is ranked nationally as the second largest, independently held, systems foodservice distributor, and it has been identified by Forbes Magazine as one of the country's "Largest Private Companies".

In addition to servicing nationwide chains, taking care of the needs of individually owned restaurants remains a strong part of their business, especially throughout New York State and the Northern Tier of Pennsylvania. Independently owned restaurants, regional chains, educational institutions, healthcare facilities and convenience stores all benefit from the talents of the Maines Account Managers. It's one-stop shopping for such establishments, since they can obtain fresh, frozen, dry grocery, paper goods, beverages, and a wide assortment of foodservice equipment. One call does it all.

The fun never ends at Maines Paper & Food Service. Have you ever watched the cooking shows on Food TV and marvel at the fascinating layout that Emeril Lagasse and others use? Believe it or not, there's a very similar setup right at the Maines Corporate Headquarters. It's a state-of the-art Learning Center and Test Kitchen that was designed in conjunction with the Culinary Institute of America and Maines own Equipment and Supply Division.

The Center is used to train both employees and customers in the use of the latest products and cooking techniques in an ever changing industry. But that's not the only way that Maines Paper & Food Service supports its restaurant customers.

They also provide publications like Mainesource Magazine, which is a menu and merchandising magazine featuring the latest products, food trends and recipes.

The slogan at Maines is "Exceptional People… Extraordinary Results". Everyone would agree that the extended Maines family is made up of exceptional people, and no one can argue with the extraordinary results which the company has achieved.

Pam Gray
Binghamton, NY

Perhaps it was Pam Gray's penchant for planning parties as a child, or her fine arts education at Syracuse University, or her love of fine food, or all of the above that brought her to the world of catering.

Pam has also always loved the "game of business", starting as a five year old selling lemonade and as a teenager working in the fast-food industry.

After college, it seemed natural to drift into the catering business. For Pam, a catering job wasn't just preparing food; it was designing all aspects of the event. From the table linens to floral arrangements to decorations and, of course, an exquisitely presented meal, Pam paid close attention to every minute detail. Her technique was to create a light-hearted, sometimes whimsical atmosphere that set her apart from others.

In the early 80's, Truffles opened. It featured cookware, imported foods, fancy candies and other hard-to-find items. It also included a restaurant, where Pam's creativity extended to the names of the sandwiches, such as Beauty and the Beef, Love at First Bite, Lox Ness Monster, Weiner and Still Champion, and Tongue Fu.

If you ever visited the original Dean & DeLuca, the gourmet shop on Prince Street in New York City, you'll have a sense of Truffles. It was cutting edge merchandising and really ahead of its time.

Pam loves the adventure of food and relishes the opportunity to try new things, especially when traveling. Always sampling what the locals are eating, she has expanded her culinary interests to include delicacies from as far away as Egypt and Morocco, where she delighted in sampling vegetarian tagines.

Today, Pam is focusing more on creating and preparing health-conscious meals, but her love for blending the culinary and visuals arts is as strong as ever.

Pat Mitchell's Ice Cream
Endicott and Binghamton, NY

In 1952, Pat Mitchell purchased a small ice cream shop from Joe Travis and began to build a legend. Pat retired in the 80's and, after a few interim owners, Tess Dzuba bought the business in 1996 and rekindled the legend. Today she operates stores in Endicott and Binghamton, both on Vestal Avenue.

Tess still uses Pat's original recipes and follows his practice of only using fresh ingredients, insisting that the cream she buys from Crowley Foods is triple pasteurized for a smoother ice cream. The fruit is fresh, the chocolate is a very special variety perfect for ice cream, and even the cookie dough is made by her from scratch for that ever popular flavor.

Her ice cream cakes are made by hand and are individually decorated. Tess will custom-decorate cakes for any occasion. Pat Mitchell's serves ice cream, sugar-free and fat-free frozen yogurt, sorbets and sherbets... but, are you ready for this, she even sells Buddy Bones. It's a milk bone ice cream sandwich so that your dog can have its own birthday celebration.

Tess' personal favorite flavor waivers between Mint Chip and Maple Walnut. Overall, the best sellers are Vanilla, Black Raspberry and Chocolate. But the kids' favorites are Crazy Cupcake, Cotton Candy and Watermelon Sherbet.

If you'd like Tess to create your own personal flavor, just let her know and she'll whip up a batch for you. In recent years, she's served garlic ice cream at the Garlic Festival and it always sells out.

Former Binghamton University students still come back to the store for their "ice cream fix", just as they did as students in years past.

Tess Dzuba has maintained the Pat Mitchell tradition and even has a new slogan "Lick the Legend," emblazed on t-shirts. Yes, the legend does live on.

Rob Salamida Company
Johnson City, NY

Rob Salamida is a perfect example of a born entrepreneur, a trait he probably inherited from his grandfather P.A. "Pat" Tierno. When Rob was 11-years-old, he sold bottles of soda to construction workers down the street from his home. By the time he was 15, he was holding down five summer jobs, including cooking and selling Spiedies in front of Jack's Delicatessen. At 16, he was calling on area businesses, selling advertising. However, he always kept his hand in Spiedie operations, branching out to serve the marinated delicacy at a variety of area establishments, using a cadre of other teenagers working for him.

Once, while on vacation with his family at the Jersey shore, Rob's father commented on what a great location the boardwalk would be for a Spiedie stand. Rob was listening intently and, as soon as they got back home, he fired off letters to New Jersey realtors asking how one might secure such a location… The reply was, "When someone dies." So much for that idea.

One evening, as he was cooking and selling in front of The Tradewinds, a stranger walked up to him and said, "Someone could make a million bucks doing this." It wouldn't be the last time he heard such a comment.

While a college student, Rob visited the New York State Fair with some friends and came back with another scheme. Why not sell Spiedies at the State Fair? Eight letters and a visit finally paid off. Fair officials agreed to rent Rob space at the end of "restaurant row". With a rental truck packed with products, he began this new adventure. Eight days later, at the end of the Fair, Rob had a net profit of $287, which was completely used to pay for a dent in the rental truck.

One Saturday morning, Rob was sweeping the sidewalk in front of his Uncle's store, Satico's. Along came Mickey Frey, his grammar school basketball coach. Mickey had some advice for Rob. "Don't fall into the trap of going to college, coming home and getting settled before you have a chance to take some risks." As the conversation turned to Spiedies, Mickey also said, "Someday someone will make a lot money selling Spiedies." The thought was not lost on Rob.

After college, Rob was intent on getting a job with one of the big New York City advertising agencies. The offers simply didn't come, but he did accept a position with Proctor & Gamble. After eight months, Rob knew the corporate world wasn't for him. He returned home, started selling advertising again, worked in his Uncle's store and, yes, went back to the State Fair. That year turned out to be a real challenge. One afternoon as the wind blew the rain horizontally, hitting him and his stand like a hail of bullets, Rob heard a voice in his head say… "Put the sandwich in a bottle."

That was enough for Rob. Back home, he started working on his first Spiedie marinade. (Until this time he had sold pre-marinated meat.) On a sheet of plywood on the family pool table, Rob created a recipe that finally satisfied him. Then it was all about marketing. He'd fill his car trunk with the marinade and call on stores all around the area.

Gradually, he was able to place his product in virtually all the local stores. Never one to just sit back, Rob began formulating State Fair Chicken Bar-B-Que Sauce. Then he created Pinch, an Italian Gourmet Spice Blend. Today Rob produces sauces and dry rubs for almost any need, including a line of products especially made for wild game. His latest addition is his own steak sauce, My Old Flame.

And for Spiedie aficionados who no longer live in this area, there's the Spiedie Survival Kit, which can be shipped anywhere in the world.

If Rob's grandfather Tierno were alive today, he'd sure be proud of this successful entrepreneur. Yes, you can make money selling Spiedies.

Southern Tier Chef's Association
Southern Tier of New York

In 1991, Chef Michael Morgan spearheaded an effort to charter a local affiliate of the American Culinary Federation. His success resulted in the formation of the Southern Tier Chef's Association, now about 25 members strong.

One of the programs offered by the Federation is a certification process for professional chefs. After passing a rigorous testing process, a successful chef may use CEC (Certified Executive Chef) after his name. If a chef has the knowledge and stamina, they can seek the Certified Master Chef designation by passing a grueling, eight-day cooking marathon.

Chefs also have the opportunity to compete against other professionals at conferences held around the country. The competition is fierce, and if you've ever watched the television show Iron Chefs on the Food Network, you'll have an idea of the challenges that they face.

Another of the Association's goals is to foster greater interest in culinary careers on the part of young people. They work closely with students in the SUNY Delhi Culinary Program. It has been honored by the National Restaurant Association for having the best two-year hospitality program in New York State. By developing an apprenticeship program for students, local Association members can be assured of another generation of creative and talented chefs.

Chef Thomas Recinalla, CEC, AAC is the incoming President of the Association and is also a Professor of Culinary Arts at SUNY Delhi. Professor Recinalla will no doubt enhance the relationship between the Association and the students even more.

You probably have seen Association members at various charitable events volunteering their time and talents. Events include those of Catholic Charities, the Boys and Girls Club, the American Heart Association, and Literacy Volunteers. The members also judge the annual Spiedie Cooking Contest.

The American Culinary Federation adopted a Culinarian's Code in 1957 and chefs around the country abide by its tenets. One rule is a pledge to advance their profession by passing knowledge and standards on to those who are to follow. Local members live the Code...every day.

Southern Tier Specialties
Barton, NY

It had never entered the minds of Jerry and JoAnn Navarro Gordon that they'd be in a food-related business when they bought a fifty-six acre parcel of land in rural Tioga County. An avid sportsman and environmentalist since childhood, Jerry was delighted to find this treasure. A variety of trees, including apple and walnut trees, coupled with open fields and a small stream, made this a dream come true.

Jerry immediately set to work planting fields with clover and other favorites of wildlife, such as deer and rabbits. He had a good idea how he wanted to improve and expand the woodlot, but engaged the services of a professional forester to be sure that he was on the right track.

He has since planted 3000 seedlings, such as red and white oak, dogwoods, cherry, elderberry, hazelnut, walnut and many others. They're carefully located to enhance the existing woodlots and fields. Jerry's work has already paid dividends in attracting a wide variety of wildlife, including a red fox, mink, weasels and, of course, deer and rabbits. When thinning the woodlot, he carefully builds wildlife habitats to attract even more species.

The apple trees hadn't been pruned in years, so one of the early projects was to cut out the dead wood and prune the trees to allow in more sunlight. The trees are thriving and there are more apples than ever for the wildlife…and a few for Jerry and JoAnn, but the side benefit was the use of the leftover branches from the pruning. A few chips of apple wood added to Jerry's charcoal grill resulted in a sweet smoking flavor that enhanced his barbecue.

If Jerry and JoAnn loved the flavor from the apple and later cherry chips, probably hundreds of people around the country would too. Soon a commercial chipper was added to Jerry's collection of outdoor toys, a logo was designed and a Website set up. Gourmet Grilling Chips were ready for the market. But Jerry and JoAnn knew that they couldn't succeed by just selling chips, so they thought about what products might appeal to the same audience.

Since he was a kid, Jerry loved "Wild Bill's Beef Jerky", which he refers to as the Jerky Connoisseur's Beef Jerky. He soon had an arrangement to be a distributor of this culinary treat. And what would a more natural addition than barbecue sauce? The famous Dinosaur Bar-B-Que Sauce from Syracuse, NY is now offered on the Southern Tier Specialties Website.

Growing up in northern New York's Adirondacks, Jerry had a favorite treat found in the local general store, namely pickled sausage, and he missed this delectable treat…until he found Zack's Pickled Venison Sausage. Jerry does have a warning though; he'll tell you that you could quite possibly sit down and eat the entire jar if you're not careful! It's available in 16 oz. jars on the Website. Gift baskets with wood chips and sauce are also available for special occasions and corporate gifts.

Jerry comes from a long line of military veterans and wanted to cater to the men and women serving our country by accommodating their desire for good beef jerky. He'll ship to APO and FPO addresses and offers a discount for those shipments with the "We Support Our Troops Special". He's now received repeat email orders from our troops in Iraq.

It's a fun business for Jerry and JoAnn, and it all started by pruning the apple trees.

SUNY Delhi Culinary Program
Delhi, NY

While SUNY Delhi isn't quite in the Southern Tier, it's only a short distance away and has a strong relationship with the Broome County area. Many local chefs are graduates of the Delhi program and there are many ties between the college and the Southern Tier Chef's Association.

Delhi offers both an Associate in Culinary Arts degree and the only Culinary Bachelor of Business Administration degree in New York State. The Associate's degree prepares students for various careers such as a Line Cook, Sous Chef, Pastry Chef or Garde Manger (a French term for "pantry", referring to the task of preparing and presenting cold food for banquets and buffets).

The graduates with a Bachelor's degree will also have training in financial management and organizational techniques to prepare them for the rigorous work of managing and running a culinary facility.

Do you remember when you last saw a custom ice sculpture? If you thought they're a thing of the past, think again. Delhi has a fully dedicated ice sculpture freezer and recently sculpted 1800 pounds of ice for a scholarship dinner.

The program hosts some of the largest culinary competitions in New York State, and Delhi students have been State Champions in the Hot Food Division six times, twice Regional Champions, and have garnered over 225 individual and team medals.

The program also operates Signatures Restaurant, a modern dining room facility. It provides opportunities for students to gain experience in a wide range of food preparation and dining room service. Friday evening features Signatures by Candlelight, where the facility is open to the public for two five-course tasting menus with specially paired wines to enhance the dining experience.

The staff in the Culinary Program is not filled with typical academics (with apologies to academics everywhere). It's not uncommon to find faculty meeting with students at 4:00 a.m. on a Saturday before a competition, coaching them to do their best.

With SUNY Delhi just 90 minutes away, it's a hidden gem in the Southern Tier. The influence which the college has on the area is far-reaching and all positive. Your next local culinary delight may have been created by a Delhi Chef.

Tom's Coffee, Cards and Gifts
Binghamton, NY

From the time he was nine years old selling bait on the riverbank, Tom Kelleher knew he'd own his own business. He worked in a variety of local restaurants and retail shops, continually thinking about opening a gourmet coffee shop. There were very few around in those days, and none in the local area.

Fate brought Tom to Lancaster, PA, where he happened across a gourmet coffee shop, The Orange Street Spice Shop. It was just like what he had dreamed about opening, and it served as his inspiration. The shop was tangible proof that the concept could work.

Tom put his business plan together and went to the bank for a loan. What the bank didn't know was that, buried in the $15,000 request, was enough money to pay for the very suit that Tom wore to the interview. The loan was approved and he opened his first shop in an area about as big as your average living room.

Like so many times over the years, Tom was a little ahead of the curve. Gourmet coffee had yet to come to its current popularity. Finding the right source for his coffee was crucial, knowing that roasting coffee beans is both an art and a science. It takes the right beans, the right temperature and the right timing…down to the second. He found a family-owned company that had been doing business for nearly half-century, and he's still doing business with them today. In 1982, his first year, he sold 900 pounds of coffee, total sales were $40,000, and he worked alone. Last year, he sold 45,000 pounds of coffee; his gross sales including gifts and gourmet food were $2 million, and he now has 45 employees.

Despite a wide selection of giftware from 350 craftspeople and a variety of hard-to-find gourmet foods, coffee is still king, with 85 varieties in stock at all times. The trends change and Tom always keeps up with the latest. About ten years ago, the sales of decaffeinated coffees were growing, but have since tapered off, and now flavored coffees are the rage. Tom's coffee roaster uses only natural flavorings, assuring his customers of the finest quality available.

One of Tom's secrets to success is his staff, whom he treats as co-workers, not employees. He takes customer service training very seriously, knowing that the customer is not an interruption of the day, but the very reason for being there.

Tom is a business owner with a social conscience. He pays his staff a livable wage and provides a full range of benefits, including health insurance that is completely paid by the company. And, the company's contributions to local charities exceed his salary.

His most recent demonstration of that social conscience is his use of 100% wind-powered energy, the first business in New York State to do so. Despite costing him more than conventionally-generated power, his commitment to protecting the environment wins out.

On his first day of business, Tom brewed a pot of his favorite coffee, Sumatra Mandheling Kasho. Ever since that time, he starts and ends his day with a cup of this same blend to remind him of where he came from.

Wagner's Cakes and Cookies
Binghamton, NY

Horst Wagner was a teenager in Germany as War II came to an end and, like many others his age, he began an apprenticeship to learn a trade. Little did he know that when he chose to learn baking he'd end up in Binghamton, NY as a renowned Master Baker.

Horst arrived in the United States in 1952, was drafted into the Army in 1954 and served for five years, stationed mostly in his native Germany. Back in the States, he first worked for his uncle in Brooklyn, and then became a partner in a bakery in Astoria, Queens.

Horst brought his special blend of Old World and New York City baking to Binghamton in 1974. He bought the old DiNarno's Bakery on Seminary Avenue in Binghamton and has been there ever since.

Horst brought many of the recipes with him from Germany. Everything is made from scratch. The eggs are fresh, it's real butter (not margarine), and you'll never find a frozen or pre-made ingredient in the Wagner bakery.

Horst is now retired, but his son, Jim, whom he began to teach when Jim was six years old, is now in charge of baking. You can find Jim's wife, Lori, behind the counter answering all of your questions. Their son Cliff is now learning the art of fine baking and, continuing the long tradition, his three year old son, Hunter, has been spotted in the bakery moving buckets around.

Wagner's breads are baked in a steam oven which guarantees a crispy crust. And, during the holiday season, the specialties can overwhelm you. For example, Wagner's offers a German bread-like cake, known as Stollen. It is usually eaten during the Christmas season and has been around since 1450.

The Wagner family takes a lot of pride in catering to ethnic preferences. Their list of specialties includes Eastern European favorites such as Paska, Buchta, and Kolache. They also produce items like Hamentaschen and Challah Bread, under Rabbinical supervision. And, if you'd like some authentic Irish Soda Bread on March 17th, just stop by Wagner's.

Their cakes and cookies remain top sellers for the bakery, and custom orders are a specialty. If you want a cake filled with half-raspberry and half-pineapple, just ask. Or, if you want a custom design, that's no problem either. For example, when President Ford visited the Fountains Pavilion, Wagner's created a cake that was a replica of the White House.

If you'd like an old photograph on top of a cake, that's no problem either. And, of course, it's edible. Another favorite is the Sacher Tort. It's chocolate laden with raspberry, and enough additional chocolate on top to satisfy any chocoholic.

Lori and her staff will also work with brides-to-be to create the perfect wedding cake. Don't worry about getting the cake to the Reception. Lori will arrange to deliver and set up the cake just perfectly.

Over 100 years of experience is baked into every cake, pastry and loaf of bread at Wagner's, all done by hand like it has been done since the beginning of baking.

Festivals and Food Related Events

Central New York Maple Festival
Democrat Women Chili Festival
Greek Festival
Senator Libous Steak Roast
The Celebration of the Feast of St. Anthony
St. Cyril's Summer Festival
St. Mary of the Assumption Annual Bazaar
St. Michael's Pirohi Sale
Strawberry Festival

Central New York Maple Festival
Marathon, NY

In 1970 a group of Marathon area residents set up a committee to organize what was then called the "Maple Syrup Festival". The original purpose was to break the monotony of Winter and to celebrate the coming of Spring. The committee's expectations were far exceeded when about 30,000 people showed up for the first festival in 1971.

About half of the village population pitched in to make it a success. Over 3,000 pancake meals were served and thousands of maple syrup samples given out. The original signs and advertising banners were created by the art classes at Marathon Central School. Oxen-drawn rides for added entertainment were part of the celebration.

The Marathon Maple Festival was now on the map. Through the years, the Festival continued to grow with horse-drawn wagon rides, antique steam engines and a variety of demonstrations from yesteryear attracting more and more people.

In 1975, the festival unveiled a new Civic Building, Exhibition Hall and Picnic Center on Lovell Field. Live entertainment and additional crafters, such as spinners, weavers and sand artists helped keep the crowd happy when not enjoying the pancakes and maple-flavored treats.

It wasn't long before train transportation was provided from Syracuse, Cortland and Binghamton. An antiques and collectible show was added, along with a juried craft show and authentic maple-sugaring exhibits.

The Festival celebrated its 25th Anniversary in 1995 with 60,000 people attending. One of the highlights that year was placing a Time Capsule in the column that supports the maple leaf plaque on the Village Green, to be opened in 2095.

The First Annual Pancake Eating Contest was held in 1997. Deputy Charlie Stevens and Fireman Craig Braman made up the winning team. Dr. Lopez was the individual winner by eating fifteen pancakes. The record holder is Joe LaRue, former Vestal resident who ate thirty pancakes in a fifteen minute time period.

A miniature petting zoo was added in 2000. In 2001 the Festival honored the late Walter Grunfeld, one of the original founders. The First Annual Maple Mobile Race was held in 2002. Students from Marathon Central School competed with soapbox derby type cars.

The honored guests in 2003 included NASA Astronaut Kenneth

Cockrell and Congressman Sherwood Boehlert. NASA Ambassador and Marathon resident Jim Rienhardt hosted a Solar System Space Exploration exhibit and displayed a Mars Rover model on loan from Cornell University. In 2005, despite heavy rains, thousands turned out on Saturday, but Sunday's Festival activities were cancelled due to the Tioughnioga River flooding the Festival grounds.

In 2006, things were back in full swing with a demonstration of dog training with Gunner, the hunting retriever, which was put on by Worthington Kennels. Another new feature was the launching of the re-designed Maple Festival Website. The NYS&W ran train excursions from Binghamton for the first time in years, catering to near capacity crowds. The excursions from Cortland were the best-attended in the history of the Festival.

Can you imagine over 11,000 pancakes being cooked and served with 110 gallons of Maple Syrup on a typical weekend? The list of maple products grows every year. Long-time favorites include maple-flavored cotton candy, maple popcorn, maple ice cream sundaes and maple lollipops. New in 2006 were maple soda and maple milk shakes.

This remarkable small town festival continues to entertain and educate maple product lovers from around the region and nation. It was even featured in the book, Best Festival Mid-Atlantic, as one of the top festivals in the Mid-Atlantic region.

For over a quarter of a century, The Central New York Maple Festival has shown Americana at its best and will no doubt continue for generations to come.

Democratic Women of Broome County Chili Fest
Broome County, NY

The "Democratic Women of Broome County" has been a prominent organization for forty years, sponsoring voter registration drives and supporting Democrat candidates for public office. Its mission is to advance the goals of the Party through public policy and political issue analysis, education, recruitment and promotion of women's issues.

But there's always time for fun too. They wanted to host an event with a modest ticket price, attract a crowd, and provide an opportunity for everyone to get to know each other better. After reviewing a number of suggestions, they decided to sponsor The First Annual Chili Fest at Brothers 2 Restaurant in Endwell in March 2006, with Lena Bishop chairing the event.

The highlight of the evening was the Chili Contest judging. The contestants included Tim Cleary, County Executive Barbara Fiala, Assemblywoman Donna Lupardo, Chairman Mike Najarian, Councilwoman Teri Rennia, City Clerk Eric Denk, Ralph Hall, Hal McCabe and Binghamton Mayor Matt Ryan.

The entries ran the range from mild to spicy, with a variety of secret ingredients. Assemblywoman Lupardo walked away with the honors and a trophy for her custom-blended Turkey Chili. The task of judging the contest went to Andrea Starzak, Barb VanAtta and Jim VonEsch, who were clearly up to the challenge.

The patrons then had a chance to sample all the Chili entries, along with corn muffins and a wide variety of desserts. With the success of the First Annual Chili Fest behind them, the club is already thinking about the next one and how to make it even more memorable

The Democratic Women of Broome County know when to be serious, but they also know that having a little fun along the way isn't a bad thing…as they'll prove again at the next Chili Fest.

Greek Festival (Νεοελληνικσ φεστιβάλ)
Vestal, NY

In 1974, the parishioners of the Greek Orthodox Church of the Annunciation in Vestal decided to celebrate their heritage and share it with the community.

They wanted authentic Greek music, dancing, costumes, artifacts and, of course, Greek food. The music is lively, the costumes exquisite and the dancing entertaining to observe, or better yet, join in. The food is inspiring. In the 70's, there wasn't much available except Gyros, Baklava and Loukoumades (Honey Puffs), beer and some Greek wines. The demand for more items exploded. Soon cooks from dozens of restaurants were volunteering their time and talents. The menu expanded to include such traditional favorites as Spanakopita, Moussaka, Pastitsio, and Dolmades, along with the Gyros and awesome desserts.

Planning for the Festival takes about three months, with on-site preparations beginning two to three weeks ahead. Ten thousand visitors on a weekend make the logistics and coordination of volunteers a huge job.

One reason that the Festival has been so successful is restaurateur Steve Anastos. Since 1975, Steve has been the driving force behind the event. He works on organizational details and leads the dancing for hours on end. Steve puts his heart and soul into sharing his love of the Greek culture.

Now there's a second generation of dancers and cooks, learning from the old-timers, some of whom have worked at the event for 30 years. The Greek Festival is a community institution which is attended by many and loved by all.

Senator Libous Steak Roast
Broome County, NY

Tom Libous took office as New York State Senator in 1989. Shortly thereafter he met with colleagues at his campaign headquarters to discuss a potential fundraising event. Tom wanted to establish a unique political function…something fun and affordable. He used as an example New York State Assemblymen "Rapp" Rappelyea's Lobster Fest held yearly in Norwich. An ordinary chicken barbecue just wasn't acceptable.

A brainstorming session devised a "Steak Roast". Tom was inspired by childhood memories of his father, a meat cutter, who would return home late from a long day of work and throw Delmonico steaks on the grill. Among the many things Tom learned from his father was a relish for that particular cut of meat and how to grill a steak like a pro.

The next step was finding an appropriate location. The only covered pavilion large enough to hold the hoped for 500 attendees was the ice rink at Grippen Park in Endicott, NY. The remainder of the menu was filled in with salt potatoes, salad and cheesecake. Tom contacted a farmer in Tioga County who had a custom built corn roaster. This began the tradition of roasted corn that has become a popular fixture at the Steak Roast.

The first year 850 tickets were sold, exceeding all expectations. Recently, the event peaked at approximately 4,000 attendees. Three huge tents have been added to the pavilion area to accommodate the crowds. People travel from all across Senator Libous' district to attend a fun evening with friends and without political speeches…a true community event.

Throughout the years a few changes were made to accommodate the growing crowds so today thousands can be served a steak dinner in about two and a half hours…an incredible 25 steaks a minute!

Hundreds of dedicated volunteers make it all happen. They set up, cook, serve and clean up...and many have been donating their time since the beginning.

Soon, Tom began thinking about making the Steak Roast even more interesting. After a lot of taste testing and research, a custom blended steak sauce was created. Friends sampled the final selections and a sauce with a rich flavor, unique texture and special ingredients…including raisin juice was chosen as the "Senator Libous Steak Sauce". The Senator admits there are secret spices and claims, "You know I can't tell you everything".

Grilling steaks at home made Tom consider adding another new product. His steaks are brought to room temperature, rubbed with extra virgin olive oil on both sides, and seasoned with salt, pepper and garlic powder. (Caution, do not season too much and overwhelm the flavor of the steak.) After grilling, the steaks are allowed to "rest" for a few minutes to allow the juices to disperse…just like his father taught him. Now he was adding his own Steak Seasoning to go along with the Steak Sauce.

Like the Sauce, he knew it had to be just right; not too much of any ingredient. More experimenting and taste testing led to the addition of Coriander to the other spices. Both the Senator Libous Steak Sauce and Steak Seasoning can be purchased each year on the third Thursday of August at Grippen Park.

The event has become legendary among politicians throughout New York State and beyond. Candidates for statewide office know that a stop at the Steak Roast is a "must". United States Senator Al D'Amato, Governor George Pataki and Mayor Rudy Giuliani are among the notables who have attended in past years. Media coverage has included USA Today, Fox News, The New York Times and many regional outlets. The Times photographer caught Mayor Giuliani enjoying a roasted ear of corn and the photo made the front page of the next morning's New York Times.

Tom's original goal for the event has been met…the Steak Roast is truly a fun, affordable and memorable occasion.

The Celebration of the Feast of St. Anthony
Endicott, NY

…Or, as some would say, La Festa di Sant' Antonio. Others simply call it the St. Anthony's Festival. Every June, for the parishioners of St. Anthony of Padua in Endicott, it's a time to work, play, welcome old friends and celebrate the life of their parish patron saint.

The celebration began in the 1930's, ceased for a few years, and was brought back bigger and better than ever a decade and half ago. The current pastor, Father Clarence Rumble, is the Festival's biggest booster. But a pastor alone doesn't make it happen. What really makes it successful are 500 volunteers who work tirelessly to host one of the community's largest events.

Food is a big part of the celebration. One station sells Lamb Spiedies, Grilled Pizza, Pizza Frites, and Pepper Cookies. Now, you may ask, what's a Pepper Cookie? It's just too delicious to explain. You'll have to visit the Festival and try them yourself, but a hint…it's an old Italian delicacy often nibbled on while sipping a glass of wine.

Food offerings include hot dogs, Pat Mitchell's Ice Cream, Italian Ice from Joey's and the many others. The "Café" serves Italian pastries, Espresso, Cappuccino, and flavored coffees.

The big draw is the main food station. Diana Ligouri and her cadre of volunteers prepare an awesome array of Italian specialties. It's worth noting that it's Diana and three other parishioners who prepare virtually all the food.

The list of offerings reads like an Italian culinary encyclopedia. From Rapini, which always sells out, to Italian Sausage, Roasted Peppers, Eggplant Parmesan, Porketta, Italian Potato Salad, Calabrese Salad, Meatballs, Chicken Spiedies, Calamari, Pasta Fagioli, Pasta with Marinara Sauce or Oil and Garlic, Grilled Eggplant, Tripe, or whatever the year's fancy strikes the cooks. The recipes are handed down from generation to generation, most of which came to America in the memories of Italian immigrants years ago.

Of course, an Italian celebration wouldn't be complete without a homemade wine-tasting competition, often pitting the younger vintners against the older. Another must-try is a taste of Joanne Michael's "Sangria Slush".

The celebration brings out young and old…from 9 months to 90 years old. They're all there to meet, greet, and…yes... eat.

St. Cyril's Summer Festival
Binghamton, NY

In 1996, a group of parishioners at SS Cyril & Method Church on Clinton Street decided to celebrate their Slovak heritage with a Summer Festival on the Parish Grounds.

In addition to games for adults and children, live entertainment and performances by the Czechoslovak Moravan Dancers in traditional costumes, there's a mouthwatering array of Slovakian foods.

Topping the edible list is Holupki, sometimes referred to as stuffed cabbage. The 8,000 Holupkis that are served to over 2,000 patrons takes a huge volunteer effort to prepare. Teams of twenty-five volunteers prepare about 1,200 Holupki at a time.

It takes 400 lbs of cabbage and 160 lbs of ground meat for each batch. The process starts with coring and steaming the cabbage, cooking the rice and sautéing the onions and celery. The rice, onions, parsley, ground meat and special seasonings are mixed together in 20-pound batches.

Then comes the tedious job of rolling the meat mixture in the steamed cabbage leaves. Once they're all rolled neatly, they're baked in tomato juice and tomato soup.

But Holupki isn't the only ethnic treat. The volunteers also prepare mounds of Haluski, which is another traditional Slovakian dish that consists of cooked cabbage and noodles. Pirohi are also available, along with Kielbasa, Sausage and Barbecued Chicken. The chicken dinners come with homemade macaroni salad and coleslaw.

Don't miss the Buchti for dessert, which are nut rolls with poppy seeds, lekvar, walnuts or apricot…and, oh, so tempting. The Zazvorniki will melt in your mouth. It's like a ginger cookie that is as light as air and is a huge seller at the festival. For an even wider selection of goodies, the parishioners also run a Bake Sale featuring homemade baked goods.

St. Mary of the Assumption Annual Bazaar
Binghamton, NY

The celebration of the Feast of the Assumption of the Blessed Virgin Mary dates back to the fifth century, and many of the Italian immigrants who settled in the neighborhoods surrounding St. Mary's Church brought their traditional forms of celebration with them. Many are still practiced, including a procession around the neighborhood displaying a tapestry depicting the Madonna. One tradition that continues to this day is the practice of pinning a dollar bill to the tapestry as it passes by.

While some things remain the same, other things change. Today, the congregation is far more diversified; one might say that it's multicultural, which has resulted in some changes to the Annual Celebration over the years. In addition to the Italian flavor of the event, you now see Irish Hibernians in the procession, as well as Irish music and dancing at the Bazaar.

People attend a bazaar like St. Mary's for different reasons. Some attend to take the opportunity to see old friends, many of whom time their visit to coincide with the bazaar, which is always on the weekend closest to the Feast Day, August 15th.

Another reason is the food…and food there is. Some of the more popular dishes include Sausage, Peppers and Onions, Pasta Fagioli, Gnocchi, Polenta, Lupini Beans, Eggplant Parmesan, and Meatballs, along with classics like Tripe and Pepper and Egg Sandwiches.

Of course, a visit to the bazaar wouldn't be complete without a stop at the dessert station to sample the Canoli, Pizzelle, Italian Cheesecake, Italian Love Cake, Pasticotti and Cripselle. Bazaar days are considered by some to be exempt from calorie counting.

It takes a lot of planning, a host of volunteers and much hard work to organize and execute such an event. Each segment has its own Chair, starting work many weeks ahead to assure that the food will be prepared, the entertainment arranged and all the logistics taken care of. They head up a cadre of volunteers which numbers close to 300, some of whom are in their 80's, and have worked the event for a half-a-century or more. It's also refreshing to often see three generations of workers at the same station.

As the only festival of its size in downtown Binghamton, it draws a wide cross-section of patrons. Everyone knows that they'll have a good time, enjoy good food and support a community institution – St. Mary of the Assumption Church.

St. Michael's Pirohi Sale
Binghamton, NY

Did you know that there's a King living here in the Southern Tier? Yes, the Pirohi King…a title Msgr. Stephen Dutko wears with pride. He's been the driving force behind St. Michael's famous Pirohi sales since he arrived in Binghamton and organized the first sale in 1964.

Msgr. Dutko had conducted successful Pirohi sales at a previous parish in Pennsylvania and knew that he could replicate those successes at St. Michael's. When he arrived, some of the parish organizations had run sales, but he knew that, if he got all the parishioners involved, it could be a huge success. Since Lenten guidelines call for parishioners to sacrifice, or "give something up", Msgr. Dutko called on the entire congregation to join in a Labor of Love and give up their time and energy to make and sell Pirohis during Lent.

He knew that success depended on volume, and hand-peeling potatoes and mixing small batches of dough just wouldn't do the job. He acquired equipment, such as a potato peeler and a commercial mixer. Over the years, the equipment has been upgraded and is now state-of-the-art and suitable for any commercial cooking operation. The mixer can handle 100 lbs of flour and 80 eggs at once, most of which are cracked by Msgr. Dutko himself. There's a roller for the dough and a machine which makes balls of the potato and cabbage filler, which are later wrapped in dough. Convection ovens cook the onions and butter sauce in record time.

Even with all of the equipment, it's still a very labor-intensive operation. One hundred and twenty five to one hundred and forty parishioners pitch in at the annual Labor of Love event. Each volunteer is provided breakfast and lunch and an end-of-day care package of Pirohis to take home. Msgr. Dutko knows that this army can't function on an empty stomach, especially when preparing food with an enticing aroma that permeates the kitchen.

The week starts with deliveries on Monday, which are unloaded from commercial delivery trucks…unlike the 1960's when Msgr. Dutko brought huge bags of flour in the trunk of his car.

On Tuesday, the onions are peeled, sliced and fried in butter. Can you imagine the tears that come with peeling 500 lbs of onions? Next, the cabbage is cored, shredded and cooked.

Wednesday is potato day. Although the mechanical peeler does a lot of the work, the eyes of 1500 pounds of potatoes must still be removed by hand. The cooked potatoes and cabbage are portioned, using the balling machine. The seasonings are simple: salt, white pepper and onion powder. The cheese must be Extra Sharp Cheddar!

On Thursday, the final production begins. Despite all of the mechanization, each Pirohi must be filled and pinched by hand, just as it has been done for centuries. A kettle steamer is used to minimize breaking and to speed up cooking. The Pirohis are dressed with the onion-butter sauce and, at last, they're ready for the throngs of hungry patrons.

The recipe for 2006 was as follows:

6,925 pounds Flour
9,450 pounds Potatoes
7,100 pounds Cabbage
2,100 pounds Onions
3,100 pounds Butter/Margarine
1,100 pounds Cheddar Cheese
15 gallons Cooking Oil
495 dozen Eggs

It's an amazing accomplishment by the Pirohi King and the entire parish. But Pirohis aren't the only thing which they cook. For special occasions and custom-orders, the same group of volunteers will whip up dozens of another Eastern European favorite: cabbage leaves stuffed with a mixture of meat and rice, baked in the oven and known as Holubki.

The annual Pirohi sale generates thousands of dollars of revenue for the parish. Perhaps more importantly, it also creates a community event for hundreds of patrons who get together for "lunch at St. Michael's" every Spring during lent.

Strawberry Festival
Owego, NY

In 1981, the Merchants Association in downtown Owego was looking for a way to promote their annual sidewalk sale. Since strawberries are a popular local crop, it was a natural marriage.

At first, it was just a sidewalk sale and a few food booths. As its popularity grew, the Festival gradually took over the entire downtown section, with streets closed and a wide variety of vendors selling their wares.

A parade was added, which includes marching bands, bagpipes, floats, antique cars, fire trucks, horses and even a politician or two. Led by the Parade Marshal and featuring the Dairy Princess, the parade is now one of the highlights of the year. The newest addition is a "pooch parade" accompanied by a dog-judging contest with proceeds going to support the local animal shelter.

Local clubs and organizations operate booths, staff parking lots and tend to other tasks. As many as 40 clubs, churches and non-profit organizations are involved, with many of them generating a significant portion of their annual budget over the Strawberry Festival weekend. The Owego Church of Jesus Christ of Latter-day Saints has taken on the responsibility for all clean-up activities as a community service. The Festival is a classic community event.

Obviously, you'll find just about every kind of strawberry dessert imaginable. Over 1,000 strawberry shortcakes are consumed throughout the day, along with hundreds of chocolate-dipped strawberries. If you're so inclined, you can surely find a strawberry daiquiri.

A new feature is a Wine with Strawberries celebration two days before the Festival. It features Wine and Food Tasting from Fingerlakes Wineries and local restaurants. Entertainment and a Silent Auction add to the gala event.

The Festival has grown to the point that a large committee oversees planning and execution. It is currently led by Pat Hansen and Karlyn Hepworth.

What started out as a sidewalk sale with a few food booths has evolved into a magnificent community celebration…a classic example of what small-town America has to offer.

Let's Reminisce

The Fountains Pavilion
The Iacovelli Family
A Look Back

The Fountains Pavilion
Johnson City, NY

As a high school student, Charlie Zades, would dash to Avenue Confectionary on Washington Avenue to help his father James. This was his first experience in a lifetime of restaurant activity. In the meantime, his future wife Jane's parents, Charles and Bessie Poulous, operated the Crystal Restaurant in Johnson City. Interestingly, James Zades would later buy the Crystal, which he operated until he sold it to Tony Tona, who recently passed away.

Charlie was an accountant by profession and Jane worked at IBM. After they married, they teamed with Guido Iacovelli to bring entertainment, such as Dick Clark's American Bandstand, Bo Diddley, The Supremes and many other famous rock 'n' roll names from the 1950's to the Endicott Johnson Recreation Center.

Then in 1964, they took over the operation of the George F. Johnson Pavilion, renamed it the Fountains Pavilion and started a legendary banquet business. It wasn't unusual to see their young children, son Jim and daughter Patricia, helping set up and clean up. Like so many family food operations, it was a guaranteed way to spend time with their parents. Later, Jim and Patricia Zades Loposky would take a more active role in the Pavilion operation when Charlie bought out his friend Guido's share of the business.

From church groups to weddings to sports and political banquets, the list of Pavilion clients is endless. Groups of a few hundred to thousands could be accommodated in the huge Pavilion space. One of the larger events was the annual St. Bonaventure Alumni Association dinner. It grew so large that the Pavilion set a cap of 1042 attendees to assure enough space between tables for the serving crew to move around easily. The Women's Abruzzese Club was another organization that packed the place every year.

The list of famous names that were honored at the Fountains Pavilion is impressive. Bobby Kennedy drew such a crowd that people were in the parking lot listening to his speech through loud speakers, and another group was tuned in at the Fountains Restaurant on the Vestal Parkway. Hubert Humphrey drew a huge crowd, and, later that evening, Humphrey's aide picked up Charlie's briefcase by mistake. It was quite a challenge to convince the Secret Service that it was OK for Charlie to swap briefcases and retrieve his own.

When President Bill Clinton visited, the crowd was even bigger, since a meal wasn't being served. The crowds were replicated when Hillary Rodham Clinton packed the house to hear her speak. When President Ford was guest of honor, Wagner's Bakery created a cake in the shape of the White

House.

The crowds were bi-partisan. Another packed house honored New York State Senate Majority Leader Joe Bruno at the Broome County Republican Committee's Lincoln Day Dinner, where patrons filled the floor and even the stage.

The food operation at the Pavilion was a sight to behold. Picture a crowd of 1,000 hungry guests looking forward to the classic family style dinner of Roast Beef, Mashed Potatoes and Gravy, Baked Ziti, Greek Cut Green Beans, Tossed Salad and a cake on the table for dessert.

Even the salads were memorable with the homemade Zades dressing. Jane would tell you that the secret to serving a great salad is to be sure that the lettuce is cold and to chill the vinegar; then add the special mixture of herbs and spices to bring out that unique Pavilion flavor.

Charlie also created an herb and spice mixture for use on prime rib, a favorite of those hosting smaller events. Other favorites included Chicken Cordon Bleu, Greek Style Stuffed Chicken Breast with homemade stuffing, and the Roasted Chicken with the awesomely seasoned roasted potatoes.

It would require twelve cooks in the kitchen, twenty servers and twelve bartenders to handle one of the big Pavilion banquets. Charlie devised a system for preparing and serving that was religiously followed. They always timed the service and the goal was to serve the entire room in twenty minutes. If you ever attended one of the Pavilion banquets, you know that they always met this goal.

Later, Charlie again teamed up with his friend Guido Iacovelli in Las Vegas. In addition to Salads Galore and Pizza Deli, they also operated Tommio's, where they introduced Spiedies to Nevada. They also operated The Vineyard, which was cited in the books ,Best Restaurants in America by Jacques Pepin and America's Best Restaurants, as an outstanding dining option in Las Vegas. The Las Vegas Vineyard had two levels, with a huge salad bar on each level. One of the many favorite menu items was the Cutlet Giovanni…a Veal Cutlet combined with homemade Manicotti.

Back in Endwell, New York, Charlie bought the Peppermill from Guido. Since the location was the same as the original Grover's Pig Stand,one of the specialties was the Pig Stand Pulled Pork Sandwich. In fact, the granddaughter of the original owner once stopped in and remarked that the sandwich was just as she remembered it from when she was a little girl.

For forty years Charlie, Jane, Jim and Patricia all made a huge mark on the local culinary scene. Although time marches on, thousands of area residents are left with fond memories of The Fountains Pavilion.

The Iacovelli Family
Broome County, NY

The Iacovelli restaurant empire started with brothers Camillo and Augostino, who was always known as Augie. They emigrated from Italy in the 1920's, Camillo to Rochester and Augie to Endicott. After Camillo married Josephine, he joined Augie in Endicott. In the 1930's, he opened a restaurant called the Parkview Terrace on the Northside of Endicott where Augie ran a catering operation and cooked at the restaurant. And, of course, this is also where the Spiedie legend began.

Camillo later opened Camillo's Spiedi Bar on the George F. Highway, and Augie opened Augie's on Odell Avenue. He sold the building to Duff Consol…and Duff's became a legend. He then re-opened on Nanticoke Avenue. Augie's wife, Rosina, who was reputed to be the best cook in the family, was a huge asset in the kitchen with her traditional Italian dishes cooked from memory.

In the meantime, Augie's sons, Guido and Tony were growing up in the business. After they both returned home from military service, the empire began to mushroom. Guido had the vision and converted Augie's into the first of many Villa Restaurants. Tony was the operations guy.

In 1957, he opened the famous Fountains Restaurant on the Vestal Parkway, near what is now the Holiday Inn. At one time, Guido left for Atlanta to try his hand at Italian fare in that southern city; Tony kept things afloat back home.

It wasn't long before Guido's vision was working overtime. In addition to the original Villa, there were others in Vestal and Binghamton. Augostino's popped up in the Oakdale Mall and The Vineyard restaurants also were becoming popular. And who can forget Coco's on the Vestal Parkway, which started out as a Disco and became a fun place for family dining? The Pepper Mill on Main Street in Endwell was also his creation. He operated what the family called the "Commissary", more formally known as Chef Italia in the "Kraft Building", on the Vestal Parkway, where huge quantities of sauce, meatballs, sausage and other Italian food products were produced.

The branching-out began with Elmira and then Ithaca. Before long there were five Iacovelli restaurants in Syracuse, three in Rochester, three in Albany, and four in Philadelphia. Next, it was off to the west to Modesto, CA, Tucson, AZ and Las Vegas, NV. With partners Anthony Mincolla and Charlie Zadcs, they opened Salads Galore and Pizza Deli, The Vineyard and Tommio's. They were immensely successful, especially The Vineyard, which was cited in the books, <u>Best Restaurants in America</u> by Jacques Pepin and <u>America's Best Restaurants,</u> as an outstanding dining option in Las Vegas. The Las Vegas Vineyard had two levels, with a huge salad bar on each level. Despite their best efforts to introduce Spiedies in Las Vegas and Modesto, apparently the residents of those cities just didn't have the educated taste buds of those living in the Southern Tier of New York.

One of the innovations tried by Guido was introducing "Italian Fast Food" at the Tommio's restaurants, both locally and in Las Vegas. It was an idea ahead of its time; customers weren't quite ready for pasta at the drive-through window.

Tony's wife, Beverly, was always actively involved. In the early days she would drive Rosina to the market for produce, and later, traveling with Tony as he oversaw various restaurants, she was always the Iacovelli right hand.

Guido had a touch for the creative. If you remember Coco's, it was a sample of "ahead-of-his-time" thinking.

With as many as thirty restaurants operating locally and around the country, it's no surprise that so many of today's cooks, chefs and restaurant owners got their start at one of Guido's restaurants.

As Guido got older, he started pulling back from the chains that he created and focused on making the Vestal Steak House one of the area's premier restaurants, which he operated until his passing.

Guido Iacovelli…as the saying goes, "A legend in his own time".

A Look Back
Southern Tier of New York

As we take a look back through time at the restaurants, diners and markets that we remember from days gone by, it's hard not to be overcome with nostalgia. Hopefully this culinary journey through the past half-century will stimulate many pleasant memories. We begin with a few classics such as Little Venice, Mary Ann's and Celeste Tavern, all lined up on Court Street…all of them had to move to make way for new highways.

Mary Ann's, which was operated by the Marianni family, moved to South Street and then to Conklin, at the same location as the Poplars. Celeste moved to Henry Street and then to the corner of Court and Carroll Streets in downtown Binghamton. Little Venice survived yet another move from its first location on Chenango Street. It is the only one of the three still in business.

Other great Italian establishments included Del Monico's, which featured steaks, seafood, Italian, and also served raw clams and oysters. There were also Del Rio, Delano's, Feeco's, Forno's, Fusco's Spaghetti Palace, Michelangelo's and Morello's. All gone, but not quite forgotten. John Robilotto operated the Silver Slipper and, at the same time Kennedy's Lounge was a popular nightclub on Fayette Street. Across from the Carlton, Crosby's was said to have the best prime rib sandwich in town. Another Chenango Street favorite was Andy Kooch's American Restaurant.

Nancy Yezzi's father, Earl Fowler, installed the first pizza oven at Cortese, and George Yezzi's aunt Carmella was a mainstay in the Little Venice kitchen for years. George also did salad prep for chef Tony Mollo at Del Monico's in the late 1940's.

There was also Milasi's Restaurant, where Nate Cortese had his first experience in the food business washing dishes. Lena and Ed Shirley operated Mama Lena's, first on Susquehanna Street and later on Upper Court Street. Tony Morabito's Mayflower Restaurant and the Brown Derby were popular places on Susquehanna Street along with the Cat and The Fiddle, operated by the immaculately dressed Frank DiBenedetto. Later, Joe Taylor occupied the location with Gentleman Joe's. Howard Hitt's Paramount Lounge was famous for its big name entertainment.

The Keg and Pitch's Oyster House were popular with the younger crowd. The Arlington and Carlton Hotels were the places to go for upscale dining and parties. Old age and urban renewal has made them just a memory. The very popular Barn Restaurant, operated by the Frieje family on

Broad Avenue, served American and Chinese food in their "Grotto". The walls were made to resemble stone…giving it a cave-like atmosphere.

The El Paso and later the New El Paso and Harry's Lunch were popular for authentic Texas Hots. Fortunately Tom Martinos has kept the tradition alive with a family recipe that has its roots at the El Paso. The Retsino Room was training ground for a number of chefs, some of whom are still plying their trade. The SDS Grill at the corner of Liberty and Henry Streets was operated by Steve DeStefano and is where long-time chef, Rocky DeSisto, got his start. Rocky worked in almost every kitchen in town at one time or another, including Little Venice, where one of his kitchen partners was Frank DeRosa. Frank can still be seen in the LV kitchen even though he's "retired". Rocky lends his cooking skills at the St. Mary's Soup Kitchen almost every day.

The Hub Delicatessen and Jewish Style Restaurant on Exchange Street was founded in 1921 by a man named Ginsberg. He moved to Washington Street and later sold it to Harry Goldman, who in turn sold it to Maxine and Philip Potchinsky, who operated it until it closed in 1975. In those days you didn't need to travel to the Carnegie Deli in New York for a bowl of Matzo Ball Soup, Kreplach Soup, or Pastrami on Rye, Chopped Herring, Bagels with Cream Cheese and Lox or Cheese Blintzes. And you didn't have to be Jewish to love the food!

In the 1950's, you'd find Oscar's, also on Washington Street, where you'd see a sign that said "No Liquors or Beers – Only Food We Serve". For many years, the place to go for ice cream was Talbot's on Conklin Avenue and on Main Street. The store served a banana split so huge that they would give a second one free to anyone who could finish the first. Hall's Ice Cream was a commercial operation on Stuyvesant Street near the river.

The basement of the then Industrial Bank Building has been home to a number of restaurants. First was The Vault, operated by Bob Guy and Dar Tiffany, which opened in 1967. Under new owners, it was later known as The Cave. It was renamed with a French twist, Le Caveau, followed by Le Chateauneuf Restaurant Francais, both of which served some very interesting continental cuisine. While their predecessors weren't greeted with much support, Mike Gennett has turned the space into a very popular Italian restaurant bearing his name, J. Michael's Restaurant and Lounge.

Dar Tiffany's Bank Café in downtown Binghamton had a unique layout. In addition to the dining room, seating was available on a balcony; and if you needed privacy for a special event you could always eat in the vault! It was known as the home of the "power lunch". Tiffany later renamed it The Paradise Café with elaborate decorative murals on the walls. After new owner, Deborah Mitchell, took over, she named it Windows. It featured a night club atmosphere in the evening.

Dino Theodoropoulos operated the Argo Restaurant on Court Street for nearly half-a-century. He started out washing dishes at the Queen Elizabeth Diner and worked his way up to a cook. In the late 1950's, he opened the Argo and operated it until his recent retirement.

Peter Metritikas was another innovative businessman. He founded the Spot, Take-A-Break and Blue Dolphin, all of which are still in business under different ownership. George and Julie Korba ran Korba's Restaurant on Lake Avenue for years. It's now Michael Alexander's.

The Boston Candy Kitchen was a downtown fixture, as was the Home Dairy, where politicians of every stripe could be seen. And who didn't love breakfast at Jim Mulcahey's Perkins Pancake House on Main Street?

The Community Coffee Shop and Lounge was another very popular establishment. Some people may remember Helen Christian, the strikingly attractive blonde hostess. It was also where John and Metro VanSavage landed their first jobs. John left the food business when he moved to Philadelphia, but Metro spent years working in the Our City of Angels Hospital kitchen in Los Angeles.

Albert Nocciolino's aunt and uncle, Venturina and Michele Nocciolino, operated Mike's Diner on State Street, and later on Court Street where Rolando's in now located.

Have you ever wondered how many people met at the Club Omar and ended up together for years? It later became the Community Lounge, joining many of the other popular nightclubs.

The Mohican Market and Bakery was owned by Francis and Ann Longo Merion in downtown Binghamton. Masciarelli's Market on Susquehanna Street was famous for its Italian sausage. Norman's and Rice's were long-time East Side fixtures.

Al and Bill Libous had AJ's Market on the Northside. Bill was a meat cutter by trade and Al was a born salesman, so they made quite a team. Al went on to become one of Binghamton's most popular mayors while Bill kept an eye on the store.

In 1915, J.K. Crowley purchased a dairy business in Poughkeepsie and moved it to Binghamton. Even though the company has changed hands through the years, its headquarters is still located in downtown Binghamton, and a processing plant functions on Conklin Avenue next to the Park Diner.

One could enjoy classic German cuisine at the Old Heidelberg, Schnitzelbank and Kiwi's. They're gone, but Rolf and Bernadette Babiel offer the same fare at Hallo Berlin in Corbettsville where Kiwi's used to be.

Ara and Harry Kradjian stepped away from their laundry and commercial real estate businesses to operate the Vestal Steak House before

146

selling it to Guido Iacovelli. They also ran Carmella's in the Giant Plaza in Johnson City. When they, along with partner Ron Kradjian, took over the Holiday Inn-Arena, they didn't want it to serve "typical Holiday Inn" food. They brought in the creative and sometimes temperamental Executive Chef Charlie Garcia and the food was mouthwatering.

On the South Side, the Kozy Korner, operated by Carmelo and Giovanna Quagliata, or, as they were better known, Charlie and Gina, was a popular Italian family restaurant until it was displaced by a highway project. Even though they offered such items as Tenderloin Steak and Veal Cutlets, the big draw was the Spaghetti and Meat Balls for fifty cents. They later opened a neighborhood grocery store, The Quality Market, on Vestal Avenue.

The Quagliata family certainly has food interests in its genes. Carmelo and Giovanna's son, John, studied hotel and restaurant management in college and took a position with Stouffer Corporation in New York City. He worked his way up to become President of the Restaurant Division and, in 1992, led a management buyout and formed Select Restaurants, Inc. John is now president of the company, which owns and operates fourteen restaurants from Boston to Long Beach, CA.

Grandson Carmen is a renowned chef in New York City's Union Square Cafe and has written the Foreword for this book, where he will recount some early food-related experiences.

One of the young waitresses at the Kozy Korner, Christine Carro, later married Pasquale "Pat" Arcodia, who opened Pino's Restaurant on Conklin Avenue. Pat always loved the opportunity to serenade the patrons with his operatic voice.

And who can forget the Fifth Ward Restaurant, Hanagan's, or "Swat" Sullivan's? In the early 1970's, the evening cook at Swat's was named Glenn. No one ever knew his last name, but everyone knew his burgers. The standard order was a ten-cent draft and a "Glennburger". Some of the regulars included Jim Herz, George Yezzi, Dick Nitto and myself when we'd head down the hill from meetings in the Town of Binghamton.

There were little places too, like Mom & Pops, a tiny restaurant just across the Court Street Bridge from downtown. For West Side residents, it was the place to stop after a Thursday evening of shopping at McLean's, Fowlers and Sisson's.

Henry's Hamburgers was selling burgers for 15 cents…those were the days! Speaking of hamburgers, up in Hillcrest, Paul Kraham was noted for his outstanding burgers at the Hillcrest Soda Spa. In the old days, he'd buy his meat fresh every day at Masciarelli's Market. The Dog House Restaurant and the New Electric Lunch were in downtown Binghamton in the 1950's.

Larry Zopp created what he called the "Zopp Burger" which he served at Zopp's Lounge on Henry Street. No one asked, "Where's the beef?" when they ordered that burger.

Remember the Alamo. That wasn't just a historic saying; it's also a reference to the Alamo Restaurants which were located on Vestal Avenue, Upper Front Street, and Upper Court Street in Binghamton and Main Street in Endwell.

Then there were the diners and coffee shops, such as the Queen Elizabeth, Tally Ho, Arrow, G&H, and Hitt's Diners. The Sun Coffee Shop, Owl Lunch, Paul's Red Hots and Ritz Tea Room added to the mix.

That Steak Place, Beaujolais, Nick's Pier7 and McCoy's Dockside all occupied the same building on Upper Front Street, which is now an office building. Slocum's Water Garden was behind LaMonica's, which later became Morey's.

In Chenango Bridge at the golf course, there was Dobb's, and then the Four Seasons. While that space now houses offices, McGirk's Irish Pub operates on the lower level.

On State Street, Anthony's was preceded by Little Italy, Hatters and Shakey's Pizza. Tommy Ryan's opened on Front Street and it later became Oliver's, then M.A. Gance's, which was operated by Tony's son Michael, now a successful caterer. A neat place was Copperfield's in the Oakdale Mall. Daniel's and Possibilities preceded Cacciatore's in the Small Mall, and The Little European on Main Street met its fate in a disastrous fire. And did you ever take your kids to the Airport to watch the planes and grab a bite to eat at the Skyview Restaurant?

Glenn Gardner made a living selling insurance, but his real love was jazz and good food. He opened the Music Box on Willow Street in Johnson City, and the jamming began. Manley Tuttle ran the kitchen and featured table-side cooking.

The Scotch 'n Sirloin was once THE place to go. One of the first restaurants to offer a salad bar, its menu was the ultimate in simplicity; just a few items pasted on a wine bottle. The original location was in the Vestal Plaza and it later moved to Plaza Drive. The chain expanded to eight restaurants in such locations as Syracuse, Buffalo and Puerto Rico. The Roaring Fork later occupied their original space and it, too, is now gone.

Tom Iacovelli now has the Plantation House which housed Le Chalet for six years and Drovers for seven. Willie Yu operated the House of Yu at the Colonial Motel long before the plethora of competition and featured Mandarin, Cantonese and Szechuan specialties. The Red Caboose was a unique setup located on Jensen Road just past the Kampai.

The Vestal Steak House survived a number of owners, but the gigantic black bull, for so long a landmark on the restaurant roof, is now out to pasture....repainted and amazing children with its size at the Discovery Center on Morgan Road in Binghamton. Emerson's Steak House, The Red Barn and Colavito's were other Vestal Parkway fixtures for a number of years.

Duff Consol was a legend on the North Side of Endicott, but his pizza was renowned throughout the Southern Tier. His family now operates Consol Family Kitchen, using many of his original recipes.

Tony Gance was another great Endicott restaurateur and his son Michael now operates a successful catering business. There was the Belvedere on Oak Hill Avenue and Masi's, where Brothers 2 is now located. Augie's was later renamed the Villa and then the Temple family operated Tiffany's at the same location.

Rossi's Market evolved from a neighborhood grocery store to the Pizza Parlor that it is now. Markos' Market was across from the Northside School and Turgiano's featured fresh fish on the weekends. Pavia and Colonna was one of the larger and more popular neighborhood stores.

The Battisti family ran the International House for years. Frank Battisti loved to cook and always wanted to operate a restaurant. With the help of his wife, Sylvia, and his sons and daughter, his dream came true. His son, Maurice was in the front of the house as the host in the white jacket, together with his wife Dianne. Frank's daughter, Donamari, a trained chef, was in the kitchen and his youngest son, Francis, was waiting tables.

Andy Mancini operated Locanda Pepina on Main Street where Nick's Pizza and Restaurant is now located.

Bucky Picciano operated Banquet Masters for years, assisted by his daughter, Tara, and is where Chef Carmen Quagliata got his start. The late, great Lampy George started at the Paradise and later moved around the corner where his protégé, Jim McCoy, operates Lampy's Mediterranean Grill, named in honor of his mentor.

Another legendary name in the business is Russ Rodriguez, who taught Jim McCoy how to cook. Russ started his career with Guido Iacovelli and worked in a number of restaurants around town. He operated Rodriguez Restaurant in Vestal and later Orlando's in Endicott where McCoy's Lampy's Mediterranean Grill is now located. This is another example of the swirl of names and locations that show the interaction of restaurateurs through the years.

Grover's Pig Stands, drive-in restaurants, owned by Stan Shawkey, were a mainstay for young and old alike. Their pork barbecue sandwiches were legendary. In addition to the restaurant on the George F. Highway, there were also Pig Stands on Main Street and Upper Court Street in Binghamton. It's where the Fata brothers got their start in the food business before opening Brothers 2.

King Arthur's was a popular eating spot on Washington Avenue and Joe Pisani's Endwell House was another must-visit establishment. There was Pizur's at Buffalo and Prescott Streets, where folks used to go for clambakes and picnics. And did you or your parents ever buy corn from Sam Arcangeli out Route 26?

Endicott Johnson Corporation originally owned and operated the En-Joie Golf Course. In 1947 John Karedes was in charge of the food operations and his son, Lou, helped out during his high school and college years. After serving two tours of duty in the military, Lou planned to teach math at UE high school. Fate intervened and in 1963 he ended up succeeding his father providing food service at EnJoie. Some of his fondest memories include meeting Babe Didrikson Zaharias when he was a kid and helping Arnold Palmer celebrate his 50th birthday when he was a participant at the BC Open. In later years, he helped play host to such luminaries as Fred Couples, John Daly and Tiger Woods. Lou is now retired, but keeps busy with volunteer activities.

The Red Lion operated under a number of owners, including the owners of the Scotch 'n Sirloin. It's still there today as Russell's Steak and Seafood House. The Russell family previously operated Surf & Turf just down the street, which was previously known as the Branding Iron Restaurant.

Thousands of people patronized the Endicott-Johnson Cafeteria and Public Market. Prices in the Cafeteria were very affordable and geared to the factory workers. The Market was years ahead of its time in offering a wide range of meats and produce.

As you reminisce about your favorite restaurants, diners and markets from years gone by, hopefully your recollections will be pleasant ones.

Good food, good times, great memories.

Venus Banquet Room

Augie's Restaurant
113 Nanticoke Ave., Endicott

Camillo's Spiedi Bar
3630 George F. Hwy, Endwell
Photo Courtesy of the Broome County Historical Society

DEL MONICO'S — The Beauty Spot of BINGHAMTON, N. Y.

Del Monico's Restaurant
161-163 Court St., Binghamton

Dan Celeste Tavern
161-163 Court St., Binghamton

FORNO'S RESTAURANT — 22 Collier St., Binghamton, N. Y.

Forno's Restaurant
22 Collier St., Binghamton

COMMUNITY COFFEE SHOP AND LOUNGE BAR
"BINGHAMTON'S FINEST"

Community Coffee Shop
Security Mutual Building, Binghamton

Henry's Hamburgers
George F. Hwy, Endwell
Photo Courtesy of the Broome County Historical Society

Grover's Pig Stand
George F. Hwy, Endwell
Photo Courtesy of the Broome County Historical Society

"Swat" Sullivan's
Vestal Ave. and South Washington St., Binghamton
Photo Courtesy of the Broome County Historical Society

Oscar's Restaurant
136 Washington Street, Binghamton

The Barn Restaurant
39 Broad Avenue., Binghamton

Del Rio Restaurant
36 Hawley Street., Binghamton
Photo Courtesy of the Broome County Historical Society

Spiedies

History of the Spiedie
History of the Spiedie Fest and Cooking Contest

The History of the Spiedie
Spiedie Fest and Spiedie Cooking Contest

Legend has it that, hundreds of years ago, as shepherds tended their flocks in rural Italy, they would butcher a lamb or goat and marinate the meat for safekeeping in a mixture of olive oil, vinegar and herbs. They would then skewer the meat on a branch from an olive tree and broil it over an open fire. The Italian word for skewer is "spiedini" and thus was born the word "Spiedie" or, as it was spelled in earlier days, "Spiedi". While that's a colorful legend, such stories have a way of being embellished over the years by writers and historians.

Here in the Southern Tier of New York, the history of the Spiedie is a bit clearer and centers around three Iacovelli brothers who immigrated from Abruzzi, Italy in the 1920's. Alphonso, while never in the restaurant business, operated a chicken farm on Upper Taft Avenue in the early 1930's. He would often invite family and friends to the farm for a picnic and served his own version of Spiedies.

Not long after, Camillo opened a restaurant known as the Parkview Terrace on Endicott's North side. Augie joined Camillo and ran a catering operation and cooked at the restaurant. He fashioned a charcoal grill complete with a fan to keep the coals hot. In the early days, Spiedies weren't marinated as we commonly do today. They were prepared with a dry rub using many of the same herbs and spices used in today's marinades. The secret touch was mopping the Spiedies as they cooked with "Zuzu", a mixture of wine vinegar, lemon juice, garlic, mint and other ingredients which are not revealed by the Iacovelli family to this day.

As a kid, Augie's son, Anthony, was often dispatched to the Bocce Court holding ten skewers of Spiedies and Italian bread and was expected to return shortly with the dollar he collected in payment.

Soon, other establishments were replicating the success of Augie's Spiedies and the food was seen in markets and neighborhood bars around the area. Camillo moved on to the George F. Highway with Camillo's Spiedi Bar and Augie opened his own establishment on Odell Avenue.

The dry rub evolved into a marinade by adding some of the ingredients used in the original Zuzu, along with olive oil. For years it was unthinkable to use anything but lamb for a Spiedie, but in the 1970's Sam Lupo experimented with using chicken for a leaner version and it was an immediate hit. Soon after, people were using pork and venison and creating their own versions of the marinade. Entrepreneurs like Rob Salamida and the Lupo family started bottling and selling their own versions of marinade locally and across the country to Spiedie-starved former residents.

In 1983, a festival was inaugurated to celebrate the Spiedie. It also provided local Spiedie aficionados an opportunity to compete in a Spiedie Cooking Contest. It has now evolved into the Spiedie Fest and Balloon Rally and attracts thousands of patrons to watch the hot air balloons launch and to feast on Spiedies. There's still a cooking contest every year, so you can still concoct your own marinade and vie for Spiedie-cooking bragging rights.

Spiedies…a local legend that lives on stronger than ever.

In the 1930's, Augie Iacovelli prepared Spiedies in front of the Parkview Terrace Restaurant on Odell Avenue in Endicott using this custom designed and built charcoal grill.

At first, he would fan the charcoal with a left-over piece of leather from the Endicott-Johnson Tannery, where he worked during the day. Looking for an easier way to bring the lump charcoal to its maximum heat, he later added the electric fan.

Augie's son, Anthony, has maintained the grill through the years and still uses it in his backyard when entertaining family and friends...just like his father and uncles before him.

History of the Spiedie Fest and Cooking Contest
Paul VanSavage

It all began one Sunday in the Spring of 1983 when I read a newspaper column by the late syndicated columnist from Chicago, Mike Royko. He was going on about the great "Rib-Fest" that was being held in Chicago's Grant Park. On the next Sunday there was another article extolling the virtues of Chicago ribs as compared with those from Kansas City or Memphis.

I wasn't able to sleep that night. I kept thinking about Royko and his ribs. Then it hit me…why not challenge Royko to bring his ribs to Binghamton? We'd have a Ribs vs. Spiedie cookoff. I wrote to Royko outlining the challenge – no answer. I wrote again and again – no answer. So I phoned him and, when he hung up on me, I knew it was time to change my thinking.

Plan B was developing in my mind. So many people in the Southern Tier area created their own version of Spiedie marinade; it seemed to make sense to have a cooking contest for Spiedies. Thus, the first Spiedie Fest was born.

The next step was to enlist a team of partners and develop a plan. The first stop was a visit with my friend Rob Salamida, the originator of State Fair Spiedie Sauce. Rob enthusiastically joined me and became co-originator of the event as well as co-sponsor.

We knew that there was a slim chance of actually making a profit on the event, so we needed a charity designated as beneficiary. A visit to Pat Millard at the offices of the American Cancer Society took care of that, along with a promise of providing volunteers.

Next on the agenda was a location. Since I worked for Broome County at the time, I was pretty confident that I could persuade my boss, County Executive Carl Young, that holding the First Annual Spiedie Fest at Otsiningo Park would be a good idea. He agreed and the Broome County Parks Department became the next co-sponsor.

I also asked County Executive Young to contact cartoonist Johnny Hart to ask if he'd design a logo. Carl glanced at me with that "When will it end, VanSavage" look, but wrote a letter to Johnny who graciously agreed to design the logo. A trip to the Hart Studio was an incredible treat. To chat with a world famous cartoonist and brainstorm with him about logo design was unforgettable. It wasn't long before Johnny had a sketch of his cartoon character, Rodney, with a Spiedie-laden spear being cooked by the fire-spewing dragon.

Now, the question was how to promote this crazy idea. Rob and

I paid a call on the folks at the Press & Sun-Bulletin. We pitched the concept of an event that would attract people of all ages, with games and entertainment in addition to the cooking contest, and they signed on as another co-sponsor and put together an incredible promotional program.

We lined up a softball game pitting the Press & Sun-Bulletin against WBNG-TV, a bocce tournament, clowns and a variety of children's games. The contest judges were an eclectic group of local Spiedie connoisseurs, who were easy to line up, since everyone in the area is a Spiedie expert. The first year judges were Dave Mack, Jim McCoy, Hal Kammerer, Bud Shumaker, Terry Holcomb, Donamari Battisti, Rick Mezzadonna, Mary Jane Battaglini, Madelaine Raichel, Ardie Masciarelli, George Yezzi, Bob Bennett, Mary Kay Liguori, and last but not least, Dave Rossie.

We had no way of knowing how many people would come out to cheer on the 65 contestants and were overwhelmed when the Parks Department count was 11,068. The first contest winners were Roxanne Bartos, Rita Leighton, and a team from Lourdes Hospital Nuclear Medicine Department. Following them were Warren Moat, Norma Mastroianni, Dan Napierala, Gloria Sullivan, John Bertoni Lena Santelli and Doug Moore.

Nearly $4000 was raised for the American Cancer Society and plans began for the Second Annual Spiedie Fest.

One of the highlights of Spiedie Fest '84 was an appearance by Augustine "Augie' Iacovelli, who some claim was the first person to cook and serve Spiedies in the area. It was another rousing success, with crowds exceeding the first year.

Shortly after the 1984 event, we were visited by Ron Rogers and Joe Slavik with a new idea. Being an avid hot air balloonist, Ron was thinking about organizing a hot air balloon rally to benefit Catholic Charities. Their brilliant idea was to build it around the successes of the Spiedie Fest.

So, in 1985, the first Spiedie Fest Balloon Rally was held at Otsiningo Park and was another overwhelming success. It has continued to grow each year and is now a weekend festival with big name entertainment and dozens of hot air balloons from all around the country.

When you visit the next Spiedie Fest Balloon Rally and watch the awesome sight of dozens of balloons lifting off, enjoy the television and recording stars entertaining the throngs, and wolf down a couple of Spiedies, remember how lucky we are to live in New York's Southern Tier.

Recipes

A collection of over fifty recipes from leading restaurants, chefs and local food enthusiasts.

A Quartet of Shrimp
Rick Dodd, PS Restaurant

Black Bean Mango Salsa and Ginger Cream

1 – 14 Oz. Can Black Beans, rinsed and dried
1 Mango, diced
1 Red Bell Pepper, diced
1 Green Pepper, diced
¼ Cup Cilantro, de-stemmed
Salt and Pepper to taste

Combine all ingredients in a bowl and mix well. Refrigerate until use.

Ginger Cream

1 Cup Mayonnaise
1 Tablespoon Ginger, diced
1 Teaspoon Dark Soy Sauce
1 Teaspoon Black Sesame Oil
1 Tablespoon Lemon Juice
1 Teaspoon Red Chili Flakes

Combine all ingredients in a bowl and mix well. Refrigerate until use.

Cucumber Yogurt Sauce with Wasabi Cream

1 Cup Plain Yogurt
2 Tablespoons Fresh Lime Juice
1 Teaspoon Chili Flakes
2 Cucumbers, peeled, de-seeded and pureed
2 Tablespoons Wasabi Powder
1 Tablespoon Water
6 Tablespoons Heavy Cream

Combine Wasabi powder and water together to form a stiff ball. Add heavy cream to Wasabi ball and whisk until smooth cream is achieved. Refrigerate until use. (You may add or subtract cream to get desired consistency)

Combine first five ingredients in a bowl and mix well. Refrigerate until use.

Asian Pesto

¾ Cup Peanuts
4 Hot Chili's, minced
3 Garlic Cloves, minced
1 Tablespoon Fresh Ginger, diced
Juice of 4 Limes
2 Tablespoons Asian Fish Sauce
½ Cup Peanut Oil
1 Teaspoon Salt
1 Tablespoon Sugar
1 Cup Fresh Mint, chopped fine
2 Cups Fresh Basil, chopped fine

Pulse all ingredients in a food processor except peanut oil, until incorporated. Add peanut oil in a steady steam while processor is running until mixture is smooth. Remove and refrigerate until use.

Avocado Puree with Chipotle Tomato Basil Sauce
Avocado Puree

2 Avocados, pitted, peeled and rough chopped
1 Hot Pepper, minced
Juice of 1 Lime
Salt and Pepper to taste
¼ Cup Fresh Cilantro, de-stemmed
1 Tablespoon Shallots, finely diced

Puree first 4 ingredients in food processor, remove to bowl. Fold in cilantro and shallots and refrigerate until use.

Tomato Sauce
6 Whole Beefsteak Tomatoes
3 Tablespoons Chipotle Pepper Powder
½ Cup Fresh Basil, de-stemmed and rough chopped
2 Tablespoons Fresh Garlic, finely diced
2 Tablespoons Olive Oil

Puree whole tomatoes in food processor until smooth. Sautee garlic in olive oil, do not let brown! Add tomatoes to oil and garlic mixture. Boil, reduce to simmer, add chipotle powder and basil and let go for 10 minutes. Remove from heat and refrigerate until use.

Shrimp

16 Shrimp, peeled and de-veined

Boil, steam, sauté or roast shrimp until translucency is gone. Keep warm until ready to plate, or refrigerate and re-warm at serving time.

Plating

Arrange your sauces on serving plates as follows:

Black Bean Mango Salsa and Ginger Cream
Cucumber Yogurt Sauce and Wasabi Cream
Asian Pesto
Avocado Puree and Chipotle Tomato Sauce

You may do this a little ahead of the serving, but not too long, as sauces may start to run out on the plate. Place your re-warmed shrimp or hot shrimp, one on each sauce combination and serve.

Other Helpful Hints

Use one large platter if you don't have a separated platter. Use assorted coatings on shrimp, like tempura, black or white sesame seeds, ground peanuts, Wasabi peas, etc. Serve shrimp cold if you like, which will give you more time with your guests. Garnish with fresh lime or lemon, fresh cilantro or fresh chives.

Akaros
Kathye Arrington

Beans are a common ingredient among African people including those of us in the west. Akaros is one of many recipes taken to the west from Nigeria during the iniquitous slave trade.

2 Cups Black-eyed peas
1 Small Spanish Onion, chopped
1 Teaspoon Salt
1 Teaspoon Black Pepper
Peanut oil

Soak black-eyed peas in water overnight, and then skin them. Combine the peas with the onion and salt and pepper and grind them in a blender or food processor. Add a little water if needed. That batter should be thin, but not soupy. Heat the peanut oil in an iron skillet to medium heat and spoon in batter with a teaspoon and fry on medium heat. Cook until golden brown on both sides. Let Akaros dry on paper towels to cool.

Now make a dipping sauce using one chopped tomato, one small onion, one tablespoon of red wine vinegar, salt and pepper. Smash them together and then you are ready to eat!

Angel Hair Salad
Michele Moelder – Health Beat Natural Foods

8 oz. Artichoke Angel Hair
¼ Cup Safflower Oil
1 ½ Teaspoon Brown Rice Vinegar
2 Tablespoons Soy Sauce
1 ½ Teaspoon Dijon Mustard
1 Large Clove Garlic, crushed
¼ Cup Fresh Parsley, chopped
Shredded Carrot
¼ Cup Chopped Walnuts

Cook pasta, drain well and set aside. Place all liquid ingredients in a jar and shake well. Place pasta in a large bowl; add walnuts, parsley and carrots. Put dressing on top and mix well.

(To lower calories in this dish, add 4 oz. more Angel Hair pasta and omit walnuts)

Asparagus Tart
Jim McCoy, Number 5 Restaurant

1 All Ready Pie Crust (half of 15-ounce package), room temperature
1 Teaspoon All Purpose Flour
14 Ounces Asparagus, each spear trimmed 3 inches long
2/3 Cup Half and Half
2 Eggs
1/2 Cup Freshly Grated Parmesan cheese (about 4 ounces)
1 Tablespoon Chopped Fresh Tarragon or 1 Teaspoon Dried
1/2 Teaspoon Salt

Preheat oven to 450°F. Open crust on work surface. Press out any cracks. Rub with flour. Arrange dough, flour side down, in 9-inch-diameter tart pan with removable bottom. Press dough into pan. Fold excess dough border over to form double-thick sides. Pierce dough all over with fork.

Bake until golden, about 15 minutes. Cool on rack. Reduce oven temperature to 375°F.

Cook asparagus in pot of boiling salted water until just crisp-tender, about 4 minutes. Drain well. Place on paper towels. Mix half and half, eggs, cheese, tarragon and salt in bowl. Season with pepper. Arrange asparagus in spoke-of-wheel fashion in crust, tips toward edge and ends meeting in center. Pour custard over. Bake until tart puffs and top browns, about 35 minutes. Cool slightly.

Avocado Havarti Burger
Paul VanSavage

Avocado Dressing

2 Ripe Avocados (preferably Hass)
2 Tablespoons Fresh Lime Juice
2 ½ Teaspoons Tabasco Chipotle Pepper Sauce
¼ Cup Fresh Cilantro, chopped

Burgers

2 lbs Ground Sirloin
1 Large Egg
½ Cup Flavored Dry Bread Crumbs
6 oz Havarti Cheese, thinly sliced

Preparing the Avocado Dressing

Peel and roughly chop the avocados. Place the avocados, lime juice, chipotle pepper sauce and cilantro in a food processor and blend until smooth. Set aside.

Preparing the Burgers

Divide the cheese into 6 equal portions. Thoroughly mix the beef, egg and bread crumbs and then divide into 12 equal portions. Form 12 thin beef patties, place a portion of the cheese on each patty, then place another patty on top and seal edges to form 6 burgers

Place burgers on an oiled grill over medium to high heat, cover and grill approximately 3 to 4 minutes on each side, depending on degree of doneness preferred.

Place cooked burger on bottom roll, top with avocado dressing, cover with roll top and serve.

Makes 6 burgers.

Avocado with Groundnut Dressing
Kathye Arrington

Ghana Vegetable Salad

2 Avocados, very ripe
1 Tablespoon Fresh Lemon Juice
2 Tablespoons Peanuts
½ Teaspoon Paprika
½ Teaspoon Cinnamon
Cayenne to taste
Salt to taste
Fresh Chives

Peel the avocados; cut out the seed and cut into cubes. Sprinkle with lemon juice and set aside. Grind the peanuts roughly with a rolling pin or in a grinder for a few seconds. Mix the peanuts and spices well. Sprinkle over the avocados with finely chopped chives. Refrigerate until ready to serve.

Baked Zucchini
Ann VanSavage

2 lbs Small Zucchini
1/3 lb Bacon, cut into pieces
Fresh Mushrooms (Optional)
3 Medium Onions, sliced
1 ½ Teaspoons Salt
¼ Teaspoon Pepper
½ Teaspoon Dry Basil
3 Tablespoons Ketchup

Wash, but don't peel zucchini. Cut into chunks or slices. Fry bacon and when almost done, add onions and mushrooms.

Put a layer of zucchini in a 1 quart casserole dish. Sprinkle with salt, pepper, basil and ketchup. Cover with a layer of onions and bacon. Repeat until casserole is filled. Finish with bacon, onions and ketchup on top.

Bake covered at 350 degrees for 45 minutes.

Serves 6.

Bavarian Meatballs (Fricadellen)
Rolf and Bernadette Babiel – Hallo Berlin

1 lb Ground Beef (not too lean)
1 lb Ground Pork
2 Eggs
3 Sliced Dried German White Bread (Crusty 2 day old)
1 Small Yellow Onion, chopped
1 Teaspoon Caraway Seed
1 Clove Garlic, crushed
1 Teaspoon Marjoram*
3 Teaspoons Yellow Mustard
Salt and Pepper to taste

Soak the bread in cold water and then squeeze out all the water. Pulse the bread, onion and garlic in a food processor until roughly chopped

Add the caraway seed, marjoram, mustard, salt and pepper to the bread mixture and pulse again until thoroughly mixed. Mix the meat, eggs and bread mixture together by hand and form large meatballs.

Add the meatballs to salted boiling water until they float to the surface. Remove the meatballs with a slotted spoon and set aside. The meatballs may be served with brown gravy or cut in half, grilled and served with mustard,

* According to Rolf, Marjoram is the key ingredient in creating the authentic Bavarian taste.

Benne Cakes
Kathye Arrington

A Kwanza Recipe

Benne cakes are a food from West Africa. Benne means sesame seeds. The sesame seeds are eaten for good luck. This treat is still eaten in some parts of the American South.

Oil to grease cookie sheet
1 Cup Brown Sugar, firmly packed
1/4 Cup Butter or Margarine, softened
1 Egg, beaten
½ Teaspoon Vanilla Extract
1 Teaspoon Fresh Lemon Juice
½ Cup All-purpose Flour
½ Teaspoon Baking Powder
1/4 Teaspoon Salt
1 Cup Toasted Sesame Seeds

Preheat the oven to 325 degrees. Lightly oil a cookie sheet. Mix together the brown sugar and butter, and beat until they are creamy. Stir in the egg, vanilla extract, and lemon juice. Add flour, baking owder, salt, and sesame seeds. Drop by rounded teaspoons onto the cookie sheet 2 inches apart. Bake for 15 minutes or until the edges are browned.

Breast of Pheasant with Dried Cherry/Pheasant Farce
Michael Morgan

2 Pheasants
1 ½ Cups Roasted Chicken/Pheasant Stock/Reduced to Glace
4 oz. Dried Cherrys, plumped in Zinfandel
4 Shallots, minced
2 Truffles, thinly sliced
2 Pheasant Livers, seared and chopped
1 Teaspoon Dry Milk
2 Tablespoons Heavy Cream
2 oz. Zinfandel Wine
2 oz. Whole Butter
12 Pearl Onions, peeled
4 oz. Assorted Mushrooms, cleaned and sliced
12 Baby Carrots, peeled and halved
4 Caraway Crackers (Please see recipe below)
4 Walnuts, pickled (Please see recipe below)
2 Cups Cabbage, shredded
4 Strips Smoked Bacon, cooked and diced
Salt and Pepper to taste
2 Apples, peeled and quartered
3 oz. Clarified Butter, for sautéing
2 Teaspoons Caraway Seed
½ Cup Apple Cider
1 Tablespoon Apple Cider Vinegar
¼ Cup Red Onions, thinly sliced
1 Clove Garlic, minced
1 Pinch Brown Sugar
4 Slices Rye Bread, crusts removed
1 Tablespoon Arrowroot Powder, mixed with stock

Remove wish bone from Pheasants. Make a slice down the back bone and loosen skin. Turn Pheasant around and make a slice down the other end and loosen breast from bone, chop off the knuckle of the leg bone and remove leg thigh meat without tearing the skin. Reserve bones for stock and cleaned meat for Farce. Remove first join from wind, clean skin off the second joint and leave intact for presentation. Each half breast should have enough skin to wrap Dried Cherry Farce into breast portion.

To Make the Farce

Chop leg thigh meat in a food processor. Sauté shallots, and garlic, add liver and cherries with wine and deglaze. Work meat and shallot together over an ice bath, add cream and dry milk, add a teaspoon of melted meat glaze, salt and pepper. Fry some of the meat and adjust seasonings. Portion out meat into the four Pheasant breasts, wrap leg thigh skin around first and fold breast skin over tightly. Slightly flatten breasts for sauté.

To Pickle Walnuts

Lightly rub off skin from whole walnuts, soak in Worcestershire Sauce overnight. The next day reduce walnuts in marinade until caramelized, but not burnt. Set aside until ready to use.

To Prepare the Cabbage

Brown apples and cook to just tender, remove from pan and set aside for presentation. Sauté red onions lightly, add cabbage, deglaze pan with apple cider and vinegar. Add caraway seeds, brown sugar, salt and pepper. Reduce liquid and taste for seasonings. Add bacon at the end to keep it crisp.

To Make Rye Cracker

Roll out bread to a thin sheet. Cut out a desired shape, brush with butter, season with Kosher salt and bake at 300 degrees until crisp, about 25 to 30 minutes.

To Cook Pheasant

Breasts; in a skillet with a fitted lid, brown breast on all sides in clarified butter, season all sides with salt and pepper and set aside. Turn the hat up and add pearl onions, carrots and mushrooms. Sauté briefly, deglaze with wine and meat glaze, set in a casserole dish, place Pheasant on vegetables, cover and bake at 300 degrees for 30 to 35 minutes, depending on over performance. Remove Pheasant, rest on a baking rack until ready to serve.

To Make the Sauce

Add all the liquid and vegetables to a sauce pan, bring to a boil and thicken with Arrowroot slurry. Finish sauce with a pat of whole butter.

To Bring the Dish Together

Divide cabbage into four serving bowls or dishes. Place two apples on top of the cabbage and one walnut on top of the apples. Slice Pheasant on a bias and rest next to the cabbage. Divide mushrooms and vegetables evenly around the four dishes. Drizzle hot Pheasant sauce around the entrees. Garnish with rye cracker.

Broccoli Normandy Soup
Diane Smith - Portfolio's Café

1 Batch White Sauce (Please see recipe below)
1 Cup Cauliflower, chopped
1 Bunch Broccoli, chopped
1 Cup Carrots, chopped
½ Cup White Onions, chopped
4 Slices Cheddar Cheese, thinly sliced

White Sauce

½ Cup Butter
½ Cup Flour
2 Quarts Milk

Melt the butter in a bowl in the microwave or a heavy saucepan. Stir in flour until all mixture is moistened. Add milk and cook, stirring until it starts to thicken.

Soup

In a heavy saucepan, combine the white sauce and all ingredients except the Cheddar cheese. When vegetables are tender, add the cheese and stir.

Broiled Salmon with Spicy Maple Basting Sauce
Jim McCoy, Number 5 Restaurant

6 Tablespoons Maple Syrup
½ Cup Water
2 Tablespoons Fresh Gingerroot, peeled and minced
2 Cloves Garlic, minced
1 Teaspoon Dried Hot Pepper Flakes, or to taste
¼ Teaspoon Salt
4 – 6 Oz Salmon Filets, about 1 inch thick

In a small saucepan combine the maple syrup, water, gingerroot, garlic, red pepper flakes and salt. Simmer until reduced to about ½ cup.

Cool basting sauce and preheat broiler. Arrange salmon skin side down on oiled rack of broiler pan. Season with salt.

Broil salmon about 4 inches from heat for 4 minutes. Bush salmon with sauce and broil until just cooked through, about 6 minutes more.

Serves 4.

Chicken and Groundnut Sauce
Kathye Arrington

5 Lbs Chicken, skinned and chopped
1 Tablespoon Nigerian Ginger
1 Clove Elephant Garlic
1 - 8oz bag of Dried Shrimp
1 - 8oz Can Tomato Sauce or Chopped Tomatoes
½ Cup of Natural Peanut Butter
2 Tablespoons Peanut Oil
½ Cup Water

In an iron skillet brown chicken with peanut until meat is cookedwell. Then set aside. Then in a sauce pan add water to the sauce pan and heat to medium. Then add shrimp to the water to soften the shrimp. Now add peanut butter, tomato sauce and mix well. Stir sauce well while grating garlic and ginger into the sauce.

Let it cook for a few minutes. Then add the sauce to the chicken and let it cook on low heat for about 20-30 minutes then serve with rice, millet or potatoes.

Chicken Cacciatore – Tuscan Style
Paul VanSavage

2 lbs Skinless, Bone-in Chicken Thighs
2 Large Baking Potatoes
2 Red Bell Peppers
4 Medium Onions
12 oz Mushrooms
2 Cloves Garlic
1 - 28 oz Crushed Tomatoes
1 - 16 oz Tomato Sauce
1 Teaspoon Dry Oregano
1/2 Teaspoon Ground Thyme

Vegetables

Peel and cut potatoes into long wedges
Clean and cut mushrooms in half
Slice peppers to approximately 1/2" X 1 1/2"
Cut onions in half and then slice
Mince garlic

Sauce

Mix crushed tomatoes, tomato sauce, oregano and thyme in a medium mixing bowl.

Browning

Brown chicken in 2 tbsp olive oil
Then brown potato wedges in the same pan

Bake

In a large casserole dish, layer the potatoes, then the chicken and then the vegetables. Pour the sauce over the mixture. Bake in a 350 degree oven for 45 minutes.

Chicken Picatta
Gary Kurz – Silo Restaurant

2 – 8 oz Boneless, Skinless Chicken Breast
3 Lemons
¼ Cup Flour
1 Tablespoon Olive Oil
1 Tablespoon Clarified Butter
2 Tablespoons Capers, drained
2 Tablespoons White Wine
1/8 Cup Chicken Broth
2 Tablespoons Beef Broth
Cooked Angel Hair Pasta
1 Tablespoon Fresh Parsley, chopped

Dredge chicken in flour. Heat the butter and oil on medium heat. Sauté the chicken on one side for approximately 4 minutes, turn over and sauté for approximately another 4 minutes.

Squeeze juice from 2 lemons. Add wine, lemon juice, capers, chicken broth and beef broth.

Simmer for 3 to 4 minutes on medium-high heat.

Serve over Angel Hair pasta and garnish with lemon slices and parsley.

Coconut Chicken
Gary Kurz – Silo Restaurant

2 – 8 oz Boneless, Skinless Chicken
½ Cup Flour
1 Cup Shredded Coconut Flakes
¼ Cup Vegetable Oil
2 Eggs

Cream of Coconut
Pineapple Juice
Cornstarch

Beat eggs in a bowl. Heat the oil in a frying pan to medium heat. Dip the chicken into flour, then the beaten eggs, and then the coconut flakes.

Sauté the chicken until golden brown, turn and brown the other side, approximately 3 to 4 minutes per side. Place in an ovenproof pan and into a 375 degree oven for approximately 8 to 10 minutes until done.

May be served with sauce of ¾ cream of coconut and ¼ pineapple juice. Heat in a saucepan and thicken with cornstarch mixed with water.

Coquille St. Jacques
Jim McCoy – Number 5 Restaurant

4 lbs Sea Scallops, 20/30 count
2 lbs Fresh Mushrooms
2 Cups Sauterne
2 Cups Heavy Cream
Juice from 3 Lemons
1 Teaspoon Ground Thyme
Paprika for color
1 Teaspoon White Pepper
24 oz. Shredded Cheddar and Swiss Cheese mixed together.
Butter/Flour Roux (See directions below)*

Cut scallops in quarters and slice mushrooms. Add wine to scallops and mushrooms and poach until scallops are about half cooked and translucent. Drain and reserve liquid.

Add heavy cram, lemon juice, thyme, paprika and white pepper to the liquid. Bring to a boil and thicken with roux. Pour liquid over scallops until well coated and place aside until desired.

When ready to prepare for serving, place 8 oz. of the mixture into a casserole dish. Top with 3 oz. of shredded cheese mixture. Bake until cheese is melted and bubbly brown.

* To make the roux, mix equal parts butter and flour in a heavy pan. Cook on medium heat, stirring constantly until the roux turns a light brown color.

Crab Stuffed Sole
Jim McCoy, Number 5 Restaurant

Crab Stuffing

2 Lbs King or Snow Crab Meat (or a combination)
1 Green Pepper
1 Medium Onion
3 or 4 Pimentos
1 Cup Mayonnaise
2 Tablespoons Worcestershire Sauce
1 Egg
Dash of Tabasco
1/2 Tablespoon Seafood Seasoning
1/2 Tablespoon Salt

Chop pepper, onion and pimento very fine. Squeeze excess water from crabmeat and crumble into vegetables. Add dry ingredients and mix thoroughly. Combine mayonnaise, Worcestershire Sauce, Tabasco and egg in separate bowl. Add wet mixture to crabmeat mixture and mix well.

Makes enough filling for 8 to 10 sole filets (or 4 to 6 crab cakes).

Sole

8 Ounces Fresh Sole, Flounder, or White fish
3 to 4 Ounces Crab Stuffing
4 Ounces Melted Butter
Slivered Almonds
Paprika

Cut fish as follows: For each serving, take two 4 ounce filets. Place the first on the bottom of your pan, and split the second along the seam. Add the filling the center of bottom filet, mold the halves over the filling. Top with melted butter, almonds and paprika. Bake at 375 degrees until brown and heated throughout.

To add Number 5's finishing touch, top with Hollandaise or Mornay Sauce.

Creamy Mushroom Soup
Charlie and Vincenzo Aiello – Aiello's Ristorante

12 oz. Button Mushrooms
6 Tablespoons Butter
½ Cup Heavy Cream
4 Cups Beef Stock
2 oz. Sherry Wine
2 oz. Burgundy Wine
2 Tablespoons Roux (See directions below)

Set aside ½ of the mushrooms. For the remaining half slice the larger one in half and leave the smaller ones whole.

In a food processor, pulse the first half of the mushrooms until very finely chopped and set aside to add later.

Melt the butter in a medium saucepan, add the whole and sliced mushrooms and sauté until tender, about ten minutes. Add the beef stock and chopped mushrooms and simmer for about ten minutes, then stir in the cream and bring to a simmer. Add small amount of roux if the soup needs thickening.

Add the Sherry and Burgundy wines and serve immediately.

Serves 4.

To make the roux, mix equal parts butter and flour in a heavy pan. Cook on medium heat, stirring constantly until the roux turns a light brown color.

Dave's Squash Bisque
Michael Morgan

4 oz. Butter
3 oz. Flour
1 quart Milk
2 Teaspoons Kosher Salt
Fresh Milled Pepper to taste
1 Pinch+ Nutmeg
1 Teaspoons Cinnamon
½ Cup Sugar
¼ Cup Maple Syrup
12 oz. Butternut Squash, frozen or Pumpkin Puree

Melt butter in a 4 quart sauce pot. Add flour and cook 5 minutes, stirring. Add milk slowly and cook to thicken. Add sugar, maple syrup, salt and spices. Taste and adjust seasonings. Add puree. thin soup with heavy cream or more mild if desired.

May be garnished with sautéed fresh apples, whipped cream, candied walnuts or croutons made with cinnamon raisin toast.

Serves 8.

Donna's Turkey Chili
Assemblywoman Donna Lupardo

2 ½ Lbs Lean Ground Turkey
2 ½ Lbs Canned Red Kidney Beans, undrained
½ Medium Onion, minced
1 Red Bell Pepper, chopped
5 Cups Tomato Sauce
2 Cans Diced Tomatoes
2 ½ Tablespoons White Vinegar
4 – 5 Tablespoons Chili Powder, to taste
¾ Teaspoons Garlic Salt
2 Teaspoons Sugar
½ Teaspoon Curry Powder

Cook ground turkey 4-5 minutes in a heavy non-reactive saucepan over medium high heat or until no longer pink stirring frequently.

Stir in remaining ingredients and bring to a boil. Reduce heat and simmer 20 minutes, stirring occasionally.

French Onion Soup
Jerry A. Temple, Jr., - Tiffany's

Soup Ingredients
10 Cups of Thick Sliced Onions
10 Cups of Water
¼ Lb. Butter
¼ Lb. Margerine
1/3 Cup Beef Base (Minor's or any good quality low salt beef base paste)
3 Tablespoons Gravy Master Browning Sauce
2 Cups Taylor Dry Sherry
1 Lb. Thick sliced Swiss cheese
1 Lb. Thick sliced provolone cheese
French Onion Soup Crocks

Croutons Ingredients
1 Loaf Day Old French Bread
¼ Lb. Margarine
¼ Lb. Butter
Black pepper
Garlic power
Onion power
Paprika
Garlic salt

Soup
Caramelize 10 cups of onions on low heat with the butter and Margarine. (Spanish onions are often used, but you may substitute red, white and yellow to make a 3-onion soup)

Add 10 cups of water, 1/3 Cup of beef base, 3 Tablespoons Gravy Master Browning sauce and simmer for 1 hour
Add 2 cups of Taylor Dry Sherry, try 1 cup taste, then another if preferred.

Add 3 Croutons to bottom of onion soup crock and cover with 1 slice of provolone and 1 slice of Swiss cheese.
Broil until cheese is bubbly and browning all around

Croutons

Melt butter/margarine blend. Dice day old French bread into 1 inch cubes Using turkey baster, wet each cube with a good dab of butter blend. Sprinkle pepper, garlic and onion power, garlic salt and paprika on wet bread cubes.

Bake in 375 degrees oven until slightly brown.

Goat Cheese Gnocchi
Michael Morgan

8 oz. Goat Cheese, softened
1 Large Egg
½ Cup Cooked Spinach, drained and chopped
1 Cup+ Flour
Salt and Pepper to taste
1 Pinch Sugar
2 Tablespoons Olive Oil
1 Tablespoon Parmesan Cheese

In a food processor, mix egg, cheese, spinach and sugar until smooth and light green. Scrape into a mixing bowl and add the flour until a semi-hard dough forms, don't over mix. Season with salt and pepper.

Refrigerate for 20 minutes before cutting dumplings. Bring 4 quarts of water to a boil, add some salt to the water.

Roll out dough with your hands to form long tubes, cut about ¾ inch pieces on the bias. Add a batch of Gnocchi to the water and cook until they float to the top.

Grilled Vegetable Casserole
Paul VanSavage

3 ½ lbs Butternut Squash, cut into 1" cubes
1 Large Red Bell Pepper, roasted
1 Large Red Onion, quartered
1 Fresh Tomato, quartered
6 Tablespoons Extra Virgin Olive Oil
3 Large Garlic Cloves, minced
3 Tablespoons Fresh Flat-leaf Parsley, minced
1 ½ Teaspoons Fresh Rosemary, minced
Freshly Ground Black Pepper to taste
Salt to taste
½ Cup Freshly Grated Parmesan Cheese
¼ Cup Plain Breadcrumbs

Preheat oven to 400 degrees F.

Roast the red peppers, let cool, peel, seed and cut into 1" pieces.

Toss the squash, onion and tomatoes with half the olive oil.

In a large cast iron or non-stick skillet, grill the squash until it starts to caramelize. Remove and set aside. Then grill the onion and finally the tomato.

In a large bowl, stir together the vegetables, the remaining olive oil, herbs, black pepper and add salt to taste.

Transfer the mixture to 2 – 2 ½ quart gratin dish or shallow baking dish. Sprinkle evenly with Parmesan. Bake until squash is completely tender, about 30 minutes.

Guinness Corned Beef with Irish Champ Potatoes
Mary Marbaker, Cooking Consultant at Olum's

Guinness Corned Beef
4 Lbs Corned Beef Brisket
1 Cup Brown Sugar
1 Can or Bottle Irish Stout Beer or Guinness

Preheat oven to 300 degrees. Rinse the beef completely and pat dry. Place the brisket on rack in a roasting pan or Dutch Oven. Rub the brown sugar on the corned beef to coat entire beef, including the bottom. Pour the bottle of stout beer around, and gently over the beef to wet the sugar. Cover and place in preheated oven. Bake for 2 ½ hours.

Irish Champ Potatoes
2 Lbs Potatoes, peeled and halved
1 Cup Milk
1 Bunch Green Onions, thinly sliced
½ Teaspoon Salt, or to taste
¼ Cup Butter
1 Pinch Freshly Ground Black Pepper to taste

Place potatoes into a large pot and fell with enough water to cover. Bring to a boil and cook until tender, about 20 minutes. Drain well. Return to very low heat and allow the potatoes to dry out for a few minutes. Mix in milk, green onions, salt and butter together until smooth.

Halibut Kabobs
Paul VanSavage

½ Cup Extra Virgin Olive Oil
¼ Cup Fresh Lime Juice
3 Tablespoons Fresh Tarragon, chopped
1 Tablespoon Fresh Oregano, chopped
2 Clove Garlic, minced
2 lbs Halibut Steak, about 1 inch thick

Trim halibut from bone and cut into 1 inch cubes.

Whisk together the marinade ingredients, adding the oil last. Reserve a portion of the marinade.

Marinade halibut for up to one hour. Grill until just cooked through, basting with reserved marinade as they cook.

Serves 4

Herb Pretzel Crusted Chicken
Bob Russell – Russell's Steak and Seafood House

Chicken Breast, boneless and skinless
Crushed Pretzels
Beaten Eggs
Olive Oil
Herbs of your choice
Broccoli, cooked
Pasta, cooked
Cheddar Cheese Sauce

Dip chicken in beaten eggs. Roll in crushed pretzels and herbs. Put olive oil in pan, add chicken and cook 7 minutes on each side at 350 degrees.

Plate cooked pasta, topped with the cooked broccoli. Place chicken breast on top of pasta and broccoli. Top with cheddar cheese sauce.

Return to oven for 4 minutes until hot and bubbly.

Honey Horseradish Bacon Wrapped Shrimp
Number 5 Restaurant

16 to 20 Large Shrimp
Horseradish
Strips of bacon
Honey

Peel and de-vein shrimp. Slice lengthwise from tip to top of tail (cut 3/4th's into the whole shrimp) Stuff with horseradish and wrap with bacon. Char-grill or sauté 3 minutes on each side.

Finish in 350 degree oven for an additional 3 minutes.

Drizzle with honey.

Insalata Caprese (Tomato Basil Salad)
Diana Ligouri – The Celebration of the Feast of St. Anthony

6 Ripe Plum Tomatoes
3 Tablespoons Extra Virgin Olive Oil
1 Small Bunch Basil
12 Small Mozzarella Cheese Balls
½ Tablespoon Wine Vinegar (Optional)
Salt to taste

Cut the tomatoes into quarters. Mix all ingredients together, adding the salt as you mix.

This salad is best served at room temperature.

Kolachky
Diane Smith - Portfolio's Café

Dough

1 lb Cream Cheese
1 lb Butter
5 Cups Flour

Filling

1 lb Walnuts, ground
1 Cup Sugar
5 Tablespoons Milk
2 Teaspoon Vanilla

Other Ingredients

Confectioners' Sugar

Work dough together with fingers; form into balls and chill. Cut dough balls in half and roll thin in confectioners' sugar. Cut into triangles.

Place nut mixture on wide end and roll, tucking in sides to seal. Bake at 375 degrees for 10 to 15 minutes.

Kulikuli (Peanut Biscuits)
Kathye Arrington

From the Country Mali.

1 Lb Roasted peanuts
¼ Cup Peanut oil, or to taste
1 Small Onion, finely chopped
1 Teaspoon Cayenne Pepper
1 Teaspoon Salt
Oil for frying

Grind or pound the nuts adding just enough oil to make a smooth paste. With wet hands, squeeze the mixture to remove any excess oil. Sauté the onions, cayenne & salt in a tablespoon of oil until golden. Knead into the nut paste. Shape into 1" diameter balls adding a few drops of water if necessary to make them hold together. Place them onto a cookie sheet coated with peanut oil and bake in the oven at 350 degrees for 10 to 15 minutes. If you like you may flatten & fry in a skillet. Cook for 2 to 3 minutes until the outsides are crisp.

Serves four.

Linguine with White Clam Sauce
Charlie and Vincenzo Aiello – Aiello's Ristorante

2 Tablespoons Olive Oil
24 Littleneck Clams
½ Cup (4 oz.) White Wine
2 Cloves Garlic
1 Tablespoon Fresh Basil, Chopped
2 Cups Chicken Stock
½ lb Linguine

Wash the clams thoroughly by placing them in a bowl of cold water and run cold water over them for five minutes.

Add the olive oil to a sauté pan and when hot add the sliced garlic. Sauté over medium heat until the garlic just starts to brown and then add the white wine.

Add the clams, chicken stock and basil. Bring to a boil, cover and simmer about five minutes or until the clams open. (Discard any clams that don't open.)

While the clams are steaming, bring a large pot of salted water to a boil. Add the linguine and cook per label instructions. Drain well, return the linguine to the pot and pour in the clams and sauce. Toss together and serve.

Lobster, Shrimp and Scallop Provencal
Gary Kurz – Silo Restaurant

2 Tablespoons Olive Oil
1 Tablespoon Garlic, chopped
½ Teaspoon Granulated Garlic
2 Pinches Salt
1 Pinch Black Pepper
1 – 4oz Lobster Tail
6 Large Scallops
1/3 Cup Sherry Wine
4 Medium Mushrooms, sliced
8 – 10 Black Olives
1 Fresh Tomato, cut into wedges
Cooked Angel Hair Pasta
1 Tablespoon Fresh Parsley, chopped

Cut lobster tail in half lengthwise. Sauté lobster in olive oil for 3 to 4 minutes on medium heat, add scallops, shrimp, chopped garlic, granulated garlic, olives, mushrooms and Sherry wine.

Cook on high heat for approximately 2 to 3 minutes. Add tomatoes and cook for approximately 1 minute.

Serve over Angel Hair pasta and sprinkle with the parsley.

Oreo Cookie Pie
Tess Dzuba - Pat Mitchell's Ice Cream

1 Prepared chocolate pie crust
½ gal Pat Mitchell's Cookies and Cream Ice Cream
½ package Oreo cookies
8 oz Fudge topping
Whipped topping

Layer ½ of the ice cream in the pie crust
Then a layer of Oreo cookies
Then a layer of the remaining ice cream
Top with fudge topping

Store in freezer. Remove 5 minutes before serving. Top with whipped topping and serve.

Pasta Fagioli
Scott Fargnoli – Donoli's Restaurant

2 lbs Ditalini
2 Cans Northern White Beans with Brine, approximately 32 oz.
2 Cans Whole Peeled Tomatoes in Juice, approximately 32 oz.
2 lbs Italian Hot Ham, cubed to bite size (Optional)
2 Cups Olive Oil
32 oz. Pasta Sauce (Your favorite)
3 Stalks Celery, chopped
1 Large White Spanish Onion, chopped
2 Tablespoons Fresh Garlic, minced
3 Cups Water
Salt and Pepper to taste

In a 10 quart or larger stock pot, add the onion, celery, garlic and olive oil. Cook on medium heat until tender, but not brown. Stir frequently to prevent burning.

Crush the tomatoes and add to cooked vegetables. Add the beans with brine, ham (optional), pasta sauce and water. heat until thoroughly hot, to a light boil.

Add the Ditalini and salt and pepper to taste. Reduce heat to low an simmer until macaroni is tender, stirring frequently. If it's too thick, add a small amount of water.

Serve with toasted French bread on the side with parmesan cheese.

Penne a la Vodka
Dominic Fata - Brothers 2 Restaurant

1 oz. Olive Oil
1 oz. Butter
1 Tablespoon Fresh Garlic, chopped
1 oz. Onion, thinly sliced
1 slice Proscuitto, julienned
1 oz. Vodka
6 oz. Marinara Sauce
3 oz. Heavy Cream
Salt Pepper to taste
2 oz. Pecorino Cheese
1 Cup Ziti, cooked

Heat a large saute pan and add oil butter and garlic. Then add the onions and Proscuitto and cook for 2 minutes.

Remove pan from heat and add vodka. Place the pan back on the heat and add salt, pepper and heavy cream. Cook for 1 minutes.

Add the Marinara Sauce, stir and add the cheese. Toss with the Ziti and serve.

Pineapple Noodle Kugel
Pam Gray

1/2 Lb Medium Noodles, cooked
6 Tablespoons Butter
1/2 Cup Sugar
1 Cup Cottage Cheese
1 Cup Sour Cream
3 Eggs, beaten
8 oz Crushed Pineapple with juice
3/4 Cup Crushed Cornflakes
1/4 Cup Sugar mixed with 1 teaspoon Cinnamon

Cook noodles, drain and add butter to hot noodles. Add eggs, sugar, cottage cheese, sour cream, pineapple and juice. Mix thoroughly, cover and refrigerate overnight.

Put in greased 7x11 baking dish, sprinkle with cinnamon sugar and flakes. Bake at 350 for 1 hour

Pumpkin Spice Cake
Mary Marbaker, Cooking Consultant at Olum's

Cake

3 Eggs, lightly beaten
1 - 15 oz. Can Solid Pack Pumpkin
1 – 18-25 oz. Package Spice Cake Mix

Combine eggs and pumpkin; whisk smoothly. Add cake mix; whisk until thoroughly blended, about 1 minute. Pour batter into microwave-safe pan, spreading evenly. Microwave cake on high for 14 minutes. Let it stand in the microwave for 10 minutes, then plate.

Glaze

1 Cup Powdered Sugar
3 – 4 Tablespoons Milk
1 Orange
12 Pecans (optional)

Combine powdered sugar and 3 – 4 tablespoons milk to make a thick glaze. Spread glaze over top of cake. Arrange pecan halves evenly and sprinkle with orange zest.

Ranch Beans
Jerry Gordon – Southern Tier Specialties

4 Cans Pork and Beans
2 Cans Kidney Beans, drained
1 lb Ground Venison (Ground Beef may be substituted)
1 lb Italian Sausage
1 lb Bacon
2 Large Onions, chopped
2 Green Bell Peppers
1 Cup Brown Sugar
¼ Cup Yellow Mustard

(Optional – A few tablespoons of hot sauce or a few hot peppers)

Stovetop
Brown ground meat and sausage and drain fat. Brown bacon (save fat), add all ingredients except beans stir and cook. Add everything to pot of beans, simmer for a couple hours.

Crock Pot
Prepare as noted above and cook in crock pot on high for 4 to 5 hours or low for 8 to 10 hours.

Rapini

Diana Ligouri – The Celebration of the Feast of St. Anthony

2 Bunches Rapini (Sometimes called Broccoli Raab)
2 Cloves Garlic, chopped
Extra Virgin Olive Oil
¼ Teaspoon Crushed Red Pepper
Salt to taste

Clean the Rapini by cutting and discarding the tough or hard stems, leaving a nice bunch of leaves and florets. Rinse thoroughly and chop roughly.

Place Rapini in a pot of salted boiling water for 3 to 5 minutes. Drain and set aside.

Add olive oil to frying pan, sauté garlic and hot pepper flakes until garlic becomes light golden. Add Rapini and cook for about 10 to 15 minutes.

Red Lentil Vegetable Soup
Michele Moelder – Health Beat Natural Foods

1 Cup Red Lentils
6 – 7 Cups Spring Water
1 – 4" Piece Kombu (Available at Health Beat Natural Foods)
2 Bay Leaves
2 – 3 Teaspoons Sesame Oil
1 Large Onion, diced
2 Stalks Celery with Leaves, diced
1 ½ Cups Chinese Cabbage, chopped (Or regular cabbage)
1 Small Butternut Squash, cubed
Herb Seasoning Salt to taste (Or sea salt)
Fresh Parsley, minced

Bring lentils, spring water, Kombu and bay leaves to a boil. Boil uncovered for 10 minutes, removing the foam which rises to the top. Sauté vegetables in the order given. Add to lentils and simmer for 15 minutes. Add seasonings and simmer for 5 to 10 minutes more. Serve warm and garnish each bowl with parsley.

Senator Libous Pasta Sauce
State Senator Tom Libous

Olive Oil
8 Oz. Proscuitto, chopped
1 Cup Scallions, chopped
1 Clove Garlic, minced
3 – 141/2 Oz. Cans Whole Tomatoes
½ Cup Dried Parsley
Salt and Pepper to taste
Cooked Pasta

Cover bottom of a saucepan with olive oil. Heat gently. Add Proscuitto scallions and garlic. Simmer for 10 minutes.

Crush tomatoes and add to pan. Season with salt and pepper.

Add parsley and simmer for 20 minutes. (Sauce should remain thin) Serve over cooked pasta.

Shells Vincenzo
Nate Cortese – Cortese Restaurant

1 lb Shell Macaroni
1 lb Ground Beef
2 1/2 Quarts Spaghetti Sauce (Your favorite)
2 lbs Whole Milk Ricotta Cheese
Romano Cheese
2 oz. Olive Oil
½ Cup Onion, chopped
4 Cloves Garlic, minced
2 Tablespoon Basil
1 Teaspoon Salt
1 Teaspoon Seasoning Salt

Pasta

Fill pot with water, add enough salt to your taste, bring to a boil and add the shell macaroni and cook for about 10 minutes. Drain water and run some fresh water in the process to rinse starch from the pasta. Put cooked and drained shells into a bowl large enough to allow mixing in spaghetti sauce and meat sauce.

Meat Sauce

Add the olive oil to a pan, sauté onion until light brown. Add the minced garlic for a minute or two and then add the ground beef. Season with basil, salt and seasoning salt as it is being cooked. Drain oil and fat from meat mixture. Add a quart of the spaghetti sauce, stir well and remove from heat.

Final Step

Add meatsauce to cooked shells using a large serving spoon to gently mix until the meatsauce is evenly distributed. Then spoon out half this mixture into a deep cake pan, forming a layer. Using a table spoon, dab out spoonfuls of Ricotta here and there on the layer. Add remainder of shells and add another layer of Ricotta. Add the extra spaghetti sauce on each layer to your liking. Sprinkle Romano cheese on top. Bake at 350 degrees until heater through.

Shrimp with Fresh Dill and Scallions
Pam Gray

2 lbs Medium Shrimp, peeled and deveined (preferably cooked at home)
1 cup Sour Cream
1 cup Mayonnaise (Regular or Light)
2 Tablespoons Chopped Fresh Dill
2 Tablespoons Thinly Sliced Scallions
½ Cup Chopped Tomato

Cook shrimp and chill until ready to use.

Mix sour cream, mayonnaise, dill and scallions. Chill until ready to use.

Just before serving, toss shrimp, sauce and tomatoes.

This dish is great for hors d'oeuvres or lunch. The sauce also works well with cooked, diced chicken.

Sloppy Joes with Chipotle
Paul VanSavage

¼ cup Red Bell Pepper – diced
2 Medium Onions – Diced
3 Cloves Garlic – Crushed
1 lb Ground Beef (Venison may be substituted)
½ lb Sweet Italian Sausage
¼ Cup Canola or Vegetable Oil
2 Teaspoons Salt
¼ Teaspoon Black Pepper
1- 15 oz Can Tomato Sauce
2-6 oz Can Tomato Paste
1 Tablespoon Chili Powder
1 Tablespoon Chipotle Chili Powder
1 Tablespoon Worcestershire Sauce

Heat half the oil in a saucepan or sauté pan over medium heat and lightly brown the ground beef. (If using venison, be careful not to overcook since it cooks quickly.) Remove the beef, drain and set aside. Repeat the process with the sausage, cook until browned, drain and add it to the beef.

Add the remaining oil to the same pan and then add the onions, red pepper and garlic and simmer until soft. Then add the chili powders, Worcestershire Sauce, salt, pepper and tomato paste. Mix thoroughly and bring to a simmer.

Add the meat and tomato sauce to the mixture, stir thoroughly and simmer for about 30 minutes.

If you prefer a less spicy version, decrease the amount of Chipotle Chili Powder.

Serve on rolls and for a different touch, try adding your favorite shredded cheese on top.

Spaghettini with Rapini, Garlic and Flaked Cod
Chef Carmen Quagliata - Union Square Cafe

8 Slices Leftover Rustic Bread, such as Pugliese
½ Cup Extra Virgin Olive Oil
1 Bunch Spring Rapini, rinsed under cold water
1 ½ Tablespoons Kosher Salt
8 Oz. Cod or Haddock, skin and bones removed, uniformly cut into six half-inch pieces.
3 Tablespoons Chopped Garlic
1 Teaspoon Dried Chili Flakes
1 Cup Dry White Wine
1 Lb. Artisanal Spaghetti or Spaghettini (such as Rustichella d'Abruzzo, Latini or Martelli)
3 Tablespoons Chopped Fresh Parsley
Juice from ¼ Lemon

Preheat oven to 300 degrees.

To prepare the breadcrumbs, place the bread slices on a baking sheet, drizzle with 2 Tablespoons of the olive oil and place the sheet in the oven. Toast the bread until golden brown, rotating the tray so the bread toasts evenly. Remove from the oven and allow to cool. Process the bread in a food processor until the crumbs are broken down to the size of grains of rice. Set aside.

Slice the Rapini cross-wise about ½ inch wide beginning at the top of the bunch and then thinner as you near the middle where there are more stems. Discard the thick stems at the bottom. Set aside.

Bring one gallon of water to a boil and season with 1 Tablespoon salt.

Season the fish with the remaining salt.

In a large sauté pan combine 2 Tablespoons of the olive oil and the chopped garlic. Place the pan over medium-high flame and cook, stirring with a wooden spoon until the garlic turns a light golden brown. Add the seasoned fish and chili flakes and continue to stir for about 20 seconds. Add the wine and bring to a boil. Turn the fish pieces and lower the flame, bring the ingredients to an easy simmer. Cook for one minute.

Using a slotted spoon, transfer the pieces of fish to a plate. They will be just cooked through and still quite moist.

Continue to gently simmer the wine broth for another 3 minutes, or until reduced by one-third. Turn off the flame.

Add the pasta to the boiling water and cook according to the instructions on the package, until al dente. Just before draining the pasta, add ¼ cup of the pasta cooking water to the wine broth. Drains the pasta well and immediate add to the wine broth.

Place the pan back on high heat. When the broth comes to a boil, add the sliced Rapini, the cooked fish and the parsley. Toss everything together gently; letting the rapini wilt and fish flake apart on its own. Taste a strand of pasta to check the seasoning for salt.

Add the lemon juice and remaining olive oil and toss. The pasta should be very moist but not too brothy. Immediately transfer the pasta to a large platter or bowl and sprinkle with the breadcrumbs.

Spanikopita
Number 5 Restaurant

1 Lb Spinach
1/4 Cup White Onion, diced
Pinch Salt and White Pepper
1/4 Cup Feta Cheese
1/4 Cup Swiss Cheese
1/2 oz Parmesan Cheese
1 Egg
Puff Pastry Squares

Sauté spinach and cheese. Let cool and drain. Season with salt and white pepper. Add remaining ingredients. Stuff puff pastry squares with ingredients.

Bake at 350 degrees for 4-5 minutes, or until tops are golden brown and flaky.

Stuffed Tenderloin
Bob Russell – Russell's Steak and Seafood House

5 oz. Tenderloin
Sliced Honey Ham
Sliced Swiss Cheese
Ritz Cracker Crumbs
Margarine, melted
Teriyaki Glaze

Pound out tenderloin thin between two pieces of Saran Wrap. Layer with ham and Swiss cheese.

Roll up and sprinkle with crushed Ritz cracker crumbs. Top with 2 tablespoons melted margarine.

Bake at 350 degrees for 15 minutes. Top with Teriyaki Glaze.

Sugarbush Fudge
Central NY Maple Festival

2 Cups Maple Syrup
1 Tablespoon Light Corn Syrup
¾ Cup Light Cream
1 Teaspoon Vanilla
¾ Cup Walnuts or Butternut Meats, coarsely chopped

Combine the maple syrup, corn syrup and cream in a saucepan. Place saucepan over moderate heat and stir constantly until mixture begins to boil

Continue cooking mixture without stirring to 234 degrees F. on candy thermometer or until a small amount of syrup forms a soft ball in cold water.

Remove pan from heat and let mixture stand without stirring unit it cools to lukewarm, 120 to 100 degrees F. Then beat mixture until it thickens and begins to lose its gloss.

Add vanilla and nuts and pour the mixture at once into a buttered pan.

When cool, cut into squares.

Summer Splendor Chicken Salad
Paul VanSavage

1/3 Cup Red Onion, finely chopped
3 Tablespoons Mayonnaise
2 Tablespoons Fresh Cilantro, chopped
3 Teaspoons Fresh Lime Juice
¼ Teaspoons Chipotle Pepper Sauce
¼ Teaspoons Salt
¼ Teaspoons Black Pepper
8 oz Grilled Chicken Breast, cut into 1" cubes
1 Large Ripe Avocado, halved, pitted and peeled

Serves 2

Mix onion, mayonnaise, cilantro, 2 teaspoons lime juice, pepper sauce in a medium bowl. Add chicken and blend well. Season with salt and pepper.

Brush avocado halves with remaining lime juice.

Arrange avocado halves, cut side up, on a bed of lettuce on serving plate. Mound chicken salad on each avocado half.

(Large ripe tomatoes may be substituted for the avocado. Slice the top off the tomatoes and remove the inside. Fill with chicken salad)

Theo's Sweet Potato Pie
Mrs. Theo
Co-Founder of Theo's Southern Style Restaurant

5 Lbs Sweet Potatoes
3 Cups Sugar
2 Cups Milk
¼ Lb Butter
4 Eggs
2 Teaspoons Lemon Extract
2 Teaspoons Nutmeg

Preheat oven to 350 degrees. Rinse potatoes and boil until tender. Cool then peel. Beat with electric mixer until all lumps are gone. Add soft butter and remaining ingredients. Mix until well blended. The mix should be same consistency as pancake batter.

Place in prepared pie shell and place on baking sheet. Bake for 1 hour or until done.

Cool before slicing, serve with love and enjoy!

Makes 2 - 9" pies

Sweet-Sour Skillet Chicken
Central NY Maple Festival

1 Broiler-Fryer Chicken, cut up
1 Cup Hot Water
¾ Cup Maple Syrup
3 Tablespoons Fresh Lemon Juice
1 Teaspoon Salt
1 Lemon, sliced
1/3 Cup Light Raisins

Arrange chicken pieces in skillet. Add water, maple syrup, salt and lemon juice. Place lemon slices on each piece of chicken. Sprinkle raisins over all. Cover tightly and cook over low heat for one hour or until chicken is fork-tender.

Three Cheese Cheesy Chicken
Bob Russell – Russell's Steak and Seafood House

Chicken Breast, boneless and skinless
Sliced Swiss Cheese
Grated Parmesan Cheese
Shredded Cheddar Cheese
Ritz Cracker Crumbs
Margarine, melted

Top chicken, first with grated cheese, then shredded cheddar cheese and then sliced Swiss cheese.

Top with crushed Ritz cracker crumbs and margarine. Bake at 350 degrees for 15 minutes.

Venison Stew
Jerry Gordon – Southern Tier Specialties

2 lbs Venison cut into 1 inch cubes
3 – 16 oz. Packages Frozen Stew Vegetables
2 – 10 oz. Cans Condensed Tomato Soup
1 Cup Water
2 Tablespoons Dried Onion Flakes
2- Large Onions
1 Teaspoon Salt
½ Teaspoon Pepper
2 Bay Leaves

Place vegetables and meat in the bottom of a crock pot. In a separate bowl mix the remaining ingredients and pour over the meat and vegetables.

Cover and cook on low setting 12 to 14 hours or on high or 3 to 4 hours.

Wild Rice Veggie Stew
Eliot Fiks – Whole in the Wall

2 ½ Cups Wild Rice
11 Cups Water
1 lb Potatoes, preferably red
3 – 5 Large Carrots
2 Medium Onions
½ Cup Soy Sauce
12 oz Mushrooms
½ Teaspoon Cayenne
½ Teaspoon Crushed Red Pepper
½ Teaspoon Sea Salt
3 Tablespoons Fresh Garlic, minced
½ lb Fresh Spinach
½ Cup Olive Oil
1 Teaspoon Cajun Spice Blend
1 ½ Tablespoons Garlic Granules
1 Tablespoon Curry Powder

Mix wild rice and water in soup pot and bring to a boil on a high flame. After boiling, cover and simmer for 40 minutes. You can begin boiling the potatoes in another pot and when they are soft, peel and chop them.

In the meantime, you can prepare your veggies. The onions should be coarsely chopped and the carrots should be peeled and cut in ¼ inch slices. The mushrooms should be cut in thick slices, and the spinach de-stemmed and coarsely chopped. After simmering the rice for 30 minutes, sauté the onions and carrots in olive oil in a separate pan. A few minutes later, add the fresh garlic to the sauté.

When the rice is done, remove and save four cups of liquid. Then, add the sautéed veggies, mushrooms, and all spices to the wild rice. Simmer another 10 minutes. During this time, in a blender, combine potatoes with remaining liquid and add to stew. Finally, add spinach, turn off flame and let sit for 5 minutes. Serve with a hunk of your favorite fresh baked bread.

Spiedie Recipes

A collection of prize-winning Spiedie recipes from past Spiedie Cooking Contest winners.

Celine's Beef Spiedies
Celine Hughes

3 – 5 lbs Tender Beef, cut into 1 inch cubes
½ Cup Wine
1 Cup Oil
Juice of 1 Lemon
¼ Cup Vinegar
2 Tablespoons Soy Sauce
5 Cloves Garlic
6 Bay Leaves, crushed
3 Tablespoons Mint Leaves
¼ Cup Parsley, chopped
1 Tablespoon Rosemary
1 Tablespoon Dried Oregano
Salt and Pepper to taste

Mix all ingredients and marinate for 3 to 4 days.

Celine's Pork Spiedies
Celine Hughes

4 lbs Cubed Pork
1 ½ Cups Olive Oil
½ Cup White Wine
½ Cup White Vinegar
Juice of 1 Lemon
5 Cloves Fresh Garlic, chopped
2 Tablespoons Fresh Mint, chopped
1 Teaspoon Black Pepper
1 Teaspoon Salt
3 Tablespoons Fresh Sweet Basil, chopped

Mix all ingredients. Add meat and marinate for 3 days.

Gloria's Lamb Spiedies
Gloria Sullivan

3 lbs Lamb, boneless, cut in cubes
3 Cups Extra Virgin Olive Oil
1 ½ Cups Balsamic Vinegar
4 Large Cloves Garlic, chopped
1 Cup Fresh Mint Leaves, chopped
¼ Cup Fresh Oregano, chopped
¼ Cup Fresh Basil, chopped
Juice of 1 Lemon
2 Packages Good Seasons Dry Italian Salad Dressing Mix
Salt and Pepper to taste

Mix marinade ingredients; add lamb and marinate. While grilling, use large sprigs of fresh mint to baste lamb with extra marinade.

Tom's Venison Spiedies
Tom Jurista

3 lbs Venison, cubed
¾ Cup Vegetable Oil
3/8 Cup Teriyaki
½ Cup Vinegar
6 Tablespoons Ketchup
5 Cloves Garlic, crushed
1 ½ Teaspoons Italian Seasoning

Combine ingredients and marinate for 2 – 3 days.

Honey Garlic Chicken Spiedies
Bob Rosati

½ Cup Virgin Olive Oil
¼ Cup Red Wine Vinegar
4 Teaspoons Season Blend (Equal parts onion powder, garlic powder, paprika, black pepper, oregano, basil, rosemary and thyme)
1 Teaspoon Salt
1 Clove Garlic
1 Red Onion
Clover Honey to taste

Place all ingredients in a blender and blend until smooth. Cover chicken cubes; refrigerate at least 48 hours. (Also good with other meats)

Hot Honey Spiedies
Bob Rosati

1 Red Onion
1 Clove Fresh Garlic
1 Teaspoon Salt
1 Teaspoon Pepper
1 Teaspoon Oregano
1 Teaspoon paprika
½ Teaspoon Cayenne Pepper
½ Cup Oil
¼ Cup Vinegar
1 Tablespoon Honey

Mix marinade ingredients in blender. Pour over pork cubes; let stand in refrigerator for at least 48 hours.

Villa-Dale Farm Spiedies
Peg and Dick Squire

1 Head Garlic, crushed
Salt and Pepper to taste
Dash Mustard
Dash Worcestershire Sauce
¼ Cup Brown Sugar
Wine Vinegar and Oil (to cover meat)
6 - 8 Sprigs Grapefruit Mint, chopped
1 Sprig Basil, chopped
3 – 4 Sprigs Oregano, chopped
2 – 3 Sprigs Italian Parsley
6 – 8 Springs Curly Mint
1 – 1 ½ Cups Chives, chopped
2 – 3 Springs Lemon Balm

Adjust ingredients until it smells like good Spiedies. Marinate leg of lamb, cubed, for 2 to 3 days. (Can also be used for chicken, beef or pork)

Greg Catlin and Julia Sansom's Chicken Spiedies
Greg Catlin and Julia Sansom

4 lbs Chicken
2 Cups Italian Salad Dressing
½ Cup Honey
2 Teaspoons Ginger
2 Teaspoons Dry Mustard
½ Cup Soy Sauce

Mix ingredients, pour over chicken and refrigerate 2 to 3 days.

Paul's Lamb Spiedies
Paul VanSavage

2 Cups Vegetable Oil
½ Cup White Wine
¼ Cup Red Wine Vinegar
1 Tablespoon Balsamic Vinegar
2 Tablespoons Kosher Salt
1 Cup Fresh Mint Leaves, chopped
¼ Cup Fresh Parsley, chopped
1 Tablespoon Fresh Rosemary, chopped
½ Cup Fresh Basil, chopped
1 Teaspoon Black Pepper
1 Teaspoon Dry Oregano
1 Teaspoon Dry Mustard
½ Cup Fresh Lemon Juice
1 Teaspoon Worcestershire Sauce
5 Cloves Garlic, crushed
1 Medium Onion, minced
1 Teaspoon Lemon Zest
5 lbs Boneless Leg of Lamb, cubed

Whisk together the wine, vinegar and salt until salt is dissolved. Add other ingredients and mist thoroughly. "Blenderize" half the marinade. Mix both batches together and marinate lamb at least 24 hours.

Index

Recipe Index

To order additional copies of Tastes and Tales of New York's Southern Tier, please contact:

Paul VanSavage
Tastes and Tales, LLC
3546 Parkway Street
Binghamton, NY 13903

Copies of Tastes and Tales of New York's Southern Tier are available at $19.95 each. Please include $1.60 NYS Sales Tax and $4.50 Shipping and Handling for a total of $26.05 for each copy. Checks may be made payable to "Tastes and Tales, LLC".

Or, you may visit ***www.TastesAndTalesSoTier.com*** and place your order online using your credit card.

Attention: Businesses and Not-For-Profit Agencies

Quantity discounts are available on bulk purchases of this book for resale, business or sales incentives, or for fund-raising purposes. For more information, please contact Paul VanSavage, Tastes and Tales, LLC, 3546 Parkway Street, Binghamton, NY 13903